CADDYING for
THE GODS

John D'Andrea

Copyright © 2015 John D'Andrea
All rights reserved
The right of John D'Andrea to be identified as the Author of the Work has been asserted by his in accordance with the Copyright, Designs and Patents Act 1988.

This book is sold subject to the circumstances that it shall not, by any way of trade or otherwise, be loaned, resold, leased, or circulated without the publisher's prior consent including any form of binding or cover other than that in which it is published and without a similar condition, including this condition, being imposed on the subsequent purchaser. Any reproduction in any form, or by any means must have the written permission of the publisher in accordance with the terms of the licenses and forms issued by the Library of Congress, Washington D.C.

Publisher: Voices Corp.

Dedication

This book is dedicated to the Siddhas and to all of those who are courageous enough to walk the Earth with light in their eyes and warmth in their hearts, and for all of those who are still lost in darkness, a gentle reminder that no one will ever be left behind…

Gratitude

Many thanks to all of my teachers, Hilda Charlton, Yogi Ramsuratkumar, Mother Meera and Reggie Ray. To Kristin Kim founder and creatress of Sansori.org , for Her Love. Inspiration and Encouragement , to Irshad Manji founder and creatress of The Moral Courage Project for Her Wisdom, Courage and Friendship. to Gloria Karpinski for Her Wisdom and Guidance to Theodora de Ridder for teaching me how to see the invisible world and to the one who is called The White Eagle, who brought this story and vision into my life for without Her none of this would have ever found form.

Foreword

Robert Trent Jones Jr.

As a golf architect, a historian, a writer, and an explorer of this journey of life, my friend John D'Andrea has captured our pursuit of an authentic life through the prism of a very ancient game that many of us have come to love. Caddying for the Gods is not an instructional book for golf but rather a fascinating journey of self-discovery. There are so many life-enriching moments and characters, and while the stories entertain they also inspire.

There is no end to the process of self-discovery, and the journey of life is a long path of learning, opening, and finding your own unique way by following your own inner guidance. Golf is a metaphor for life, and Caddying for the Gods has captured the true spirit of this journey. Enjoy your travels.

The wisdom within this book is a gift from an old friend…

ONE

They say things work out the way they're supposed to, but often it's not the way we've planned. This could be the credo of my life. I've never been too much of a planner; I have some direction, sure, but just enough to get me to my short-term goals. Then, once I'm there, I like to see what will happen next. No commitments, no constraints, just me and fate staring one another down, waiting to see who flinches first.

I guess that sort of explains how I ended up in Scotland in 1984, driving around in a car with a guy from Australia. If that sounds like the setup for a joke, that's because in a way it is. Not the stale, random kind of joke that one often hears on a golf course; more like the cosmic sort of joke that continues to unfold right up until today, one that always seems to put me in the right place at the right time to move my life forward. This guy—Lance was his name—and I had met while scouting out the grounds of the tiny Leven Links golf course that is nestled along the east coast of Scotland. A few days earlier, I'd been on my way to Paris to visit some friends, but a young assistant golf pro had called me just as I was leaving and asked me to caddy for him in the qualifying round for the British Open. So I took a detour, and we met up in Scotland.

At the time I was pretty young, too, just twenty-one years old, but I'd been around the game of golf since I was a child. I grew up in Westchester, New York, and had a friend who was a member at the Winged Foot Golf Club, one of the most famous golf courses in the world. It's been around since 1923, and membership is by invitation only. This friend, his grandfather used to take us there when we were eight years old to fish in one of the ponds. Then he'd buy us lunch, and we'd eat out on the terrace of the clubhouse and watch the many golfers wander by.

A few years later, when I was twelve, I'd started to caddy at Winged Foot to make a little pocket money—and, in all honesty, to create a little space between my parents and me. I'd been immediately drawn to the those wide-open spaces and fields of green that in many ways gave me the opportunity to experience a deeper freedom, though I didn't know at the time how far and how deep those fairways and that freedom would ultimately lead me.

The game of golf has always fascinated me. It's so individual—just you and the ball and all of the many thoughts and emotions that go into making up who you think you are. I can still remember the first time I caddied and how I struggled with the bag. It was for an elderly woman who had to be at least eighty, but I could hardly keep up with her; luckily for me she played only nine holes. I don't think I would have made the full eighteen. I knew very little about golf back then and even less about caddying. All I knew was that you followed somebody around, carried their clubs, and tried to stay out of the way. Then you got paid. It seemed like a good deal to me. At the very least it was a means to an end.

And that was (and is) how caddying has remained to me: as the tool through which I have enabled myself to live the life I've wanted—or, I suppose, the life that the gods have somehow sent in my direction. Mostly that's amounted to traveling around the world, which is a great coincidence because that's all I ever really wanted to do since I was a kid. My earliest memories of my childhood are of hearing the sounds of a freight train off in the distance and dreaming that someday I would see the world. Larchmont was nice and all by materialistic standards, but it wasn't exactly exotic, and I could never really buy into the idea of a one-way ticket to the suburbs. As a result I invested as little as possible into the realities and belief systems I had inherited from my ancestors. Instead I daydreamed about white-sand beaches and snowcapped mountains and ancient cities and everything in between, not to mention all the people out there who were not like me, people who would teach me the things I needed to know. Of course I had no idea what I needed to know back then, and I still don't. Who ever does? But there was a big, wide world out there calling me, and I was determined to do everything I could to answer it.

Anyway, back to Lance.

"Have you ever been to Thailand?" he asked out of the blue, glancing over at me from his seat behind the steering wheel. We'd just left Leven Links and were driving north on the A915 through the evening mist. I could just make out the North Sea to the east, out beyond the wild fescue grasses that swayed gently in the wind and the postage-stamp greens of one of the many golf courses in the area. Lance was giving me a ride to St. Andrews, where we were both staying. In the passenger's seat, I was busy rolling a joint with some grass I'd smuggled in with me from California.

"No. What's in Thailand?" I asked him with a smile. I liked this carefree guy and his random questions. We were like two long-lost brothers who were somehow picking up where we'd left off last time around. When I'd first arrived at Leven Links that morning, I'd caddied for my pro in a practice round and then gone back out on the course to walk off some yardages. Back then there were no sophisticated measuring devices like we have today; there weren't even sprinkler heads to measure from. I had to be pretty creative in finding reference points like old divots, an occasional stone here or there, little mounds in the earth, or the crest of a ridge that I would mark off with some neighbor's door in the nearby village just to be sure I could return to that same point once the tournament began. I'd find one then walk from there to the front edge of the green and count my steps. That was my yardage.

Of course it was pouring rain that day, which would make finding those points even more challenging than usual. But it had to be done. So I grabbed an oversize umbrella from the pro shop and headed out. I was just coming up to the first tee when I saw another guy coming in the opposite direction. He was pushing what looked like a small wheel attached to a metal stick. I'd never seen anything like it before.

"G'day," he said with an Australian accent and a friendly nod as he approached the tee.

"Hey," I said back, looking at that strange device of his. "Can I ask you a question?"

He was busy writing something down in the pad he carried with him, but he had no umbrella, and the pages were soaking wet. He gave up, looked at me, and shrugged. "Sure."

I pointed at the stick. "What is that?"
He held it up a little and looked at it. "That's a yardage wheel," he said. "For measuring distances, so you don't have to do the old heel-to-toe dance all over the place." Then he laughed and nudged me a little with his elbow.

I got the joke, and I got how good this yardage wheel of his was. I imagined the amazing amount of time it would save.

"Listen," he said. "You share that umbrella with me, and we can chart the course together with this thing." He lifted the wheel again and shook it a little.

How could I say no to that? Not only could I come up with more-accurate yardages, but I'd also have a companion from the other side of the world who obviously knew a lot more than I did. So I agreed, and we measured and charted the entire course in just a few hours. Then we headed into the clubhouse to dry off in front of the fireplace and get lost inside a bottle of local whiskey.

"In Thailand there's this island," he continued now, as he maneuvered his rental car down the road. "Or rather off the coast of Thailand, in the south. Koh Phangan, it's called. I've gone there on holiday sometimes, stay for as long as I can—one, two months, three if I'm lucky." He looked over at me intermittently as he spoke, a wide grin on his face, one hand waving through the air while the other gripped the steering wheel.

"The place is a paradise," he went on. "Turquoise beaches with no one around for miles…skies so clear it feels like you could reach up and grab the stars. Everything runs on generators, and they turn 'em off at ten every night, so all the lights go out, and it's just you and the darkened universe out there in the middle of nowhere."

He paused, gazing out at the road, his mind obviously a thousand miles away. I didn't say a thing, just waited for him to go on.

"It's a very special place. Only those who are willing to turn their backs on the many modern illusions of safety and security are able to find their way into this Garden of Eden. And the people—they're so laidback. So gracious, no matter where you're from. They're descended from sea gypsies, I heard, and you can totally see it. They're real bohemian. No schedules, no stress, no worries…"

I laughed then I licked the rolling paper of the joint I'd rolled and pressed gently to seal it shut. "That does sound like paradise." It also reminded me of my days out on the road with the Grateful Dead, where the only time we paid attention to was when the next show would start. There were no days, no weeks, no months, just one continuum of adventure.

"It is," Lance went on, his voice growing quiet and serious. "It's a place untouched by the world. How many of those are left?" He sighed. "Would be a shame if it ever got really discovered."

A silence filled the car, and I let it envelope us, warm and comfortable like an old sweater on this still rainy day. I looked out the car window; the North Sea was receding, now just a dark mass in the distance. Earlier I'd stood on its shore, watching the shallow, slate-blue waves lap along the rocky coast. As far as bodies of water went, it was nice to look at, I gave it that. But it certainly wasn't the most dramatic I'd seen. My mind flashed back now to the shores of Hawaii, where I'd spent some time caddying a few years earlier. Waves there crested at eighteen feet and rolled into whiteheads on the beach, pounding it with the thunder of a god. Then my thoughts moved on to the Monterey Peninsula, where I've seen whales migrating down the coast from the tees of Spyglass Hill while I was caddying. Finally there were the cliffs of La Jolla, where I had watched hang gliders fly over me and weave their way through the sky as I caddied on Torrey Pines.

Prior to all of that, I'd been in Miami attending college, believe it or not. I even paid my own tuition from the money I'd saved from caddying. But after a few short months, I'd quickly realized what they were trying to teach me would be of no use to me in the world in which I wanted to live. Theorems and hypotheses, algorithms, literature written by old white men who died centuries ago…what did that have to do with me? Nothing, I believed, and I came to see the college experience as one big waste of my hard-earned money.

However, in those three short months, I did discover one thing: the Grateful Dead. I'd heard their music before and thought it was okay, but it wasn't until a friend took me to see them live in Hollywood, Florida, that I realized there was a whole 'nother level of experience there waiting to be explored. The lights, the sound, getting lost in this enormous traveling circus of like-minded folks, the improvisational nature of it all—it was so intoxicating I couldn't pass it up. Two nights later I found myself in the lobby of an old hotel right across the street from the Fox Theater in Atlanta. The Dead had just wrapped up their tour with a performance that people still rave about today. The scene in the hotel was equally magical: hundreds of hippies and Dead Heads had taken over; someone had dosed the bartender, so drinks were on the house; and there were orange peels raining down from the balconies like snowflakes from all of the plantations we had raided on our way north. After that eventful evening there was no way I could ever go back to the life I had once lived. It was time to drop out of one world and enter another.

School and I quickly parted ways, and I headed back to New York to gather whatever resources I had left. Then I traveled on to California to caddy on the PGA Tour but more importantly to see the Dead on New Year's Eve in Oakland. And that, I guess, was the one that sealed the deal. I did manage to caddy in a few tournaments on the PGA Tour, but right after that I boarded an old converted school bus and toured the country with the Grateful Dead, following them (along with hundreds of other loyal fans) from town to town and show to show. The Dead were known for their nonstop touring, but occasionally they did take breaks, and when they did, I did too. I'd head back to Mamaroneck to caddy at Winged Foot. I'd save up the money I earned, and in a few weeks I'd be back on the road again, catching up to the band and my newfound friends wherever they were. I'd just been heading out on one of these breaks when the young pro called me about the British Open. And now there I was, staring out at the North Sea, realizing that as soon as this job was over, I'd be on a plane to Thailand.

TWO

Lance had been right about Koh Phangan: it was a paradise on Earth. As I was coming up to the island by boat, my breath was literally taken away by the postcard-perfect image of the place: the water a luminous turquoise, the shore a concave of sugary-white-sand beaches framed by tall, verdant palm trees. The mountains rose out of the sea, surrounded on the land by a lush rainforest. These, I would later learn, were the uninhabitable areas. Forty percent of the island was a national park that would always be protected from development.

Most Koh Phangan denizens lived close to the coast. With a view like that, I thought, I couldn't blame them. Throw in a warm breeze and a hammock, and I'd be set for the rest of my life. Or so I thought.

The boat I was on was coming in from Ko Samui, another small island in the Gulf of Thailand. Back then there were no piers on Koh Phangan, so the boat had to anchor a few hundred yards offshore, and a smaller vessel—a refugee boat that had made its way there from Vietnam during the war—came out to collect the passengers a few at a time.

That small boat, to prevent getting grounded, would not go

all the way to shore but would drop the visitors off in the water when it was about knee deep. Then we waded the rest of the way in. It was a lot of work, and it took forever to get us all on dry land, but in many ways it acted as a filter that kept out the jet-set tourist crowds who were more interested in showing off their fancy watches and designer suitcases than appreciating the beauty of nature surrounding them.

The moment I set foot on the island, I saw that Lance had also been right about the origins of the people there. They were clearly gypsies, with a wildness in their eyes that reflected the freedom of their spirits, which could never be claimed by any one nationality. On the beach a group of local residents greeted me with warm and friendly smiles and welcomed me with the little English they had learned along the way.

This was no sales pitch, no travel-agent recitation of brochure-ready jargon. These were just people talking to me as a person. They reminded me of the folks I'd met while on the road with the Grateful Dead—so unselfish, so unaware even of their own egos. All they wanted to do was talk and hear something good, something positive. To help someone if they could.

I hadn't been on Koh Phangan for five minutes, and already I felt like I was a member of the tribe, like I had just returned home, back to a life I had once lived and loved but forgotten about for a while. Fate had certainly brought me there; consider as evidence the last-minute phone call from the golfer, the detour to Scotland, my meeting Lance and his yardage wheel. In this instant it all made sense to me, and I was reminded once again that things have a way of fitting together whether we realize it's happening or not. These pieces had been falling into place all along; I just hadn't been paying attention.

The more I paid attention, the more I realized that our

destinies stretch out from us like spun threads, taut and twanging like guitar strings with every move we make, with every metaphorical corner we turn. They stretch and weave into other people's strings for a while if we're lucky. The problem is we never know when some unseen hand will decide to give our strings a twist or even a cut that will send us reeling in a totally different direction than we'd planned.

It was already late afternoon by the time I'd arrived, and it would be getting dark soon. While sleeping out on the beach underneath the millions of stars that would soon be sprinkled throughout the sky seemed like a great idea to me, my new friends advised me that it wasn't wise. The tide came in at night, washing the sand clean and taking any debris back into the gulf with it. I would be among that flotsam, they told me good naturedly. Then they suggested that I head toward the eastern tip of the island and pointed to a lighthouse on top of a hill. There were some houses for rent up there. They helped me arrange for a small boat that would take me in that direction.

And that was where I lived for the next eight years, just below the lighthouse in an open-air, Balinese-style house that looked out on to the Gulf of Thailand and the many smaller national park islands that were scattered out to the west.

Day-to-day life on the island was just about as throwback as you'd want it to be, like time stopped there a thousand years ago. Early in the morning, just at dawn, I could see the silhouettes of fishermen setting out into the gulf in their longboats, plying the trade of their ancestors. The island's coconut farmers use methods that had been handed down to generation after generation. Both fishing and this type of farming were really the only local industries, and they supported the local economy—what there was of one. Most things I needed could be bought for a song. Everyone on the island, myself included, lived on fresh papaya and bananas, drank coconut water, and either bought fish from the villagers or went out and caught their own.

Back then there were no roads on the island, so people traveled either by foot or by longboat, and despite all the walking, no one wore shoes. On many of the beaches, no one wore clothes very much either. Keeping with the bohemian nature of the place, many of the foreign inhabitants survived on money they made from selling clothes, jewelry, and hashish they would bring in from Manali. And there were parties on the beaches every night. We smoked grass smuggled in from Laos, and every once in a while someone got their hands on a bottle of liquid LSD, and the whole island, it seemed, would be dosed for a week. It was easy to tell when there were psychedelics in town because everything—trees, rocks, faces—somehow got covered in Day-Glo paint.

With this sort of lifestyle, no one ever really knew what day or month it was. No one needed to—that was the beauty of it. We literally were, as Lance had said, in the middle of nowhere. These were the pre-Internet days, so there was no regular contact with the outside world. No one had a cell phone, and there was no such thing as texting; you actually looked someone straight in the eye in order to communicate. Every once in a while, I would find a week-old newspaper left behind in a restaurant, but other than that the entire Earth outside Koh Phangan's perimeter was a rumor at best.

Lance's stars—yeah, they were a real thing. The island was so far out at sea, there was no light pollution like you get in any of the big cities or even small towns at times, clogging up the sky and reducing any visibility you might have down to nothing. After the generators shut off on Koh Phangan, everything was pitch dark and, unless you were at a party, completely silent. I loved that amazing sense of stillness and often found myself just standing outside to enjoy it.

Many nights I would stumble home in the wee hours of the morning after a party, always stopping to watch the glow of fluorescent plankton at the tops of the small waves that broke on the shore. When there was a full moon, the island glowed with a milky-white light that was bright enough to read by but not to drown out the heavens. I can remember one clear night when I grabbed a book and headed down to a rocky area of the shoreline, where I settled on the flat top of a boulder. I read for a while and then lay down on my back, hands folded behind my head, and marveled at all of the beauty that surrounded me. Up above the Milky Way stretched from one end to the other as far as I could see, millions of stars literally splashed across the sky. The star system Sirius would change colors before my eyes, from red to sea blue and then to white. Venus, the brightest body in the sky after the moon, stood out with such clarity, it felt closer to me in distance than my home back in Larchmont. I stared at it for what felt like hours until the image of it was burned into my eyes even after I closed them.

#

Koh Phangan was a haven for drifters, dropouts, and dreamers. I was probably a little bit of all three at that time in my life (and in many ways still am). I was still young, still had no idea where I was going in life, nor did I really want to know. I was okay with going wherever the tide took me. My childhood dream of immersing myself in other cultures and meeting new and interesting people all around the world had become a reality, and that was good enough for me at the moment. If and when fate decided it was time for me to be somewhere else, I'd move on. Until then the life that I had stumbled into was exceeding my wildest imagination.

Whereas some people might find existence on a tiny island monotonous and boring, I believe that our experiences in any place that we occupy on the game board are entirely what we make them. And I was determined to make my stay on Koh Phangan as pleasurable as possible. It wasn't hard to do when almost every day was about eighty degrees and sunny. There was a wet season, as it was known, when monsoons were regular occurrences, toward the end of each year, but those were great times as well. I would collect as much rainwater as possible in the many tanks I had surrounding my house, to use later for drinking and showering—there's nothing like taking an outdoor shower in fresh rainwater. Sometimes it was nice to get off the beach and just spend some time inside, reading a book and listening to the rain prance—or sometimes pound—on the roof overhead.

Most days, though, the weather was good, and I and everyone else on the island would spend as much time as possible outdoors. There were plenty of beaches, all of them beautiful and serene; some were so secluded you could go for hours without seeing anyone. There were the mountains, too, in the center of the island, rising up green and lush out of the forest. Within them were many hidden waterfalls that my friends and I would seek out; they had been formed during the rainy season and would disappear within only a few months.

The island was governed by trade winds that would shift about every six months. I could always tell when it happened by the fragrance of the breeze. The winds blew in from China in the northeast from Malaysia and Indonesia in the southwest. The latter were warmer and as a result more fragrant.

Whether you were into hiking and exploring or lying in the sun all day and doing nothing, Koh Phangan had a little something for everyone. One of my favorite things on the island was a tai chi school that sat on the other side of a hill just behind my house, on the cliffs overlooking the water. Most people gravitated there at one time or another to balance out the nonstop partying. The school was called the Heart of the Dragon; it offered instruction of the tai chi form in two sessions every day for four weeks. I had never tried to learn it before, but I had seen it done—twelve years earlier, in 1981, while touring Europe with the Grateful Dead. They'd been playing on the outskirts of Paris, and I was coming in on a train from Germany that afternoon to check out the scene before the show.

While stopped in a café for lunch, I ran into a guy I knew—ironically, a Dead Head from Berlin whom I had met some months earlier in Berkeley, California, when the Dead were doing a show at the Greek Theater. We left the café and headed to a nearby park, where we lay in the grass and shared a smoke to celebrate our good fortune of making it to Paris to see another show and finding one another again. At one point he got up and wandered a little way down the grass then he stopped and struck a pose—standing with his feet shoulder width apart, knees slightly bent, arms hanging at his sides with his elbows sticking out a little bit. He breathed deeply and gazed unfocused out across the park.

Then he raised his hands. First dragging them up in front of his body slowly, wrists and fingers lax. At about chest height, he lifted his hands and pushed, palms out, until his arms were almost fully flexed. Then, with his forefingers and thumbs almost making a triangle shape in front of him, he brought his hands down again, farther out this time, and started the round all over again.

Round, I thought. That was how the movement looked. As if

he were running his hands around a very large ball.

After doing that for a while, he went on to a series of other poses, moving so slowly and smoothly it had a lulling effect even on me. This exercise, whatever it was, looked so graceful, so serene, I almost wanted to jump up and join him, to get in on this peaceful experience. But instead I just sat there, watching in awe from across the lawn.

Finally he came back, a big smile on his face.

I handed him the smoke I'd been holding. "Hey, what was that?" I asked.

He inhaled, held it in, let it out in a long, slow stream. "Tai chi," he answered. "The supreme ultimate state of undifferentiated, absolute, and infinite potential." Then he smiled wider.

I really liked the sound of that. And later on I got him to teach me a few moves. I got the gist of them but could tell this wasn't something you could learn how to do in an hour or even in a day. It took steady practice and much patience. I put it on my list of things to explore one day.

That day came on Koh Phangan, when I found the Heart of the Dragon. I signed up for classes, which, to my good fortune, started the next day. And I went, twice a day, through the entire four-week course. I had been correct—patience and practice were the keys here, along with learning how to let go of all the moorings I still had in my life to the many unconscious patterns that in many ways dictated my posture and my reality as well. In tai chi there are no things; there's no money to worry about or social status to look after. There is you, your spirit, and the energy you carry with you through life and the many movements you make along the way.

Back in Paris, watching my friend from Berlin start his tai chi routine, I had been right: those hand movements had been tracing out a ball shape in front of him, but I now learned that the ball was not imaginary. It was made of energy, and it was real. Sometimes in class we would stand in that first pose—called the Wuji stance—for quite some time and run our hands around and around, warming ourselves up in a way but also awakening that energy within ourselves. The more I focused on my movements, the more I could feel it, like a spring that was bubbling up inside of me, and the gentle pressure from the empty air in front of me. The energy was a real thing, a physical entity I could touch but not see.

The four weeks of that class changed me. Though I'd thought I'd been at peace before, I reached a new level of calmness and acceptance of not just the way things were but the way they could be and the ways in which I had to let them happen. I'd known this all along, that the gods, fate—call it what you will, but there was some universal force that pushed me in the direction I was supposed to go. Now I also knew there was this energy that I had to take along with me wherever I went. It was not mine, though; I was merely borrowing it.

On the last day of the tai chi class, when I had completed learning the entire form, I left the school feeling a little melancholy. Of course I could and would continue practicing the form on my own; in fact I would work it into my routine at least once a day to help me focus and relax. But I would miss the school. I sat outside it for a little while before heading home, on the cliff overlooking the water, surveying this magical island paradise I had come to call my home. The water, the sand, the trees, and as I looked up into the hills to my right, I saw what I thought was a stranger making his way down the path toward the school. I watched him make his way down, a tall, thin figure with dark hair and—

No, it couldn't be. I squinted and brought my hand up to shade my eyes from the bright sun. For a moment there, this guy had looked like…well, he looked like the Dead Head I'd met up with in Paris twelve years earlier, the guy from Berlin who had planted that seed of tai chi in my soul. Could it be possible? That we would both be on this tiny island now and outside the tai chi school both at this very moment?

No, I believed in fate, of course, and still do; in my travels I've found there are no coincidences, just things that happen to move us along down the rivers of our lives, on to the next port where we're meant to dock at least for a while. But this—this was just too odd to be true. Still, I saw this man stop to talk to someone, and this familiar, big, wide smile spread across his face.

I had to ask.

I jumped up from my spot on the cliff and hesitantly walked over toward him. When he was done with his conversation, I approached.

"Excuse me," I said. "Are you…are you from Berlin? I know it's an odd question."

The man looked at me for a moment, eyes squinted as if trying to discern what my motive was.

"Were you in Paris about twelve years ago?" I went on, feeling more confident now that I was up close that this was really him.

Another moment of scrutiny, and then in an instant his expression changed. His face opened up, the smile returning. "John? Is that you?" He sounded just as amazed as I felt.

After we got over just how much this unlikely reunion blew both our minds, I took him back to my house, and we stayed up all night just talking and catching up on where the last decade had led us. He had become a Buddhist monk, ordained in Thailand, and was just now returning from Burma, where he had practiced meditation for several years.

"But you're not wearing a robe," I noted. He was dressed just like me, in loose pants and a T-shirt, typical island garb.

"I disrobed a few months ago," he explained, "so I can reenter the stream of my former life with all the new tools I've learned and a very different insight into the nature of reality."

That set us off on a whole other tangent of conversation: What was reality? Was it what we saw and heard and tasted? Or did it exist only in our minds? Was my reality the same as his or the same as anyone else's on Earth? Despite all his studies, he didn't have the answers, of course; no one ever does. But there was one thing on which we could agree: all the practices we undertake, all the disciplines we follow, they are all just different paths designed to bring us closer to the lives we are supposed to lead, the lives we are given by the powers that be. The challenge, then, is to heed that call and have the courage to set out upon that road when it's presented to us.

#

During my eight years on the island, I did escape once in a while and head back to New York, where I would caddy for a few months and make enough money to live on for a lot longer than that. Then I'd head back to my sanctuary, far away from so-called proper society. The more time I spent outside the everyday rat race that 90 percent of the "civilized" world seems to run on a daily basis, the stronger my conviction that it was not an exercise I enjoyed. I made money because I needed to; Koh Phangan was a paradise, yes, but I still had to pay for a few things like rice, fish, and fruit. The difference was I did not make excess money just to have, just to put into a bank account where it would turn into nothing but phantom numbers that somehow were supposed to help me sleep at night. That's all money is, really: a ghost. It haunts everyone at some point, whether they have it or not. The rich man obsesses about his and worries that it will one day leave him, whereas the poor man dreams about it night and day and wonders if it will ever find its way into his life.

Easy to say things like this when you live on a speck of land in the middle of an ocean, right? I know. But it doesn't make it any less true. And it only made it more painful when money finally began to find its way to my adopted home's shores.

I'm not quite sure exactly when it started—maybe around my seventh year there. Little by little things changed on the island. First there were more new people coming in than usual, and they did not all have the same respect we locals did for the land and the indigenous culture that had been there for more than two thousand years before we showed up. In many ways the next wave of tourists reminded me of some of the people I had caddied for over the years: mentally confused, spiritually lost, arrogant souls who brought with them all the illusions and demands of their egocentric lives. The rich and shameless, as I like to call them, came to Koh Phangan for a week or two, muddied up the collective psyche then went back to their lives full of shiny, modern conveniences.

This caused the whole dynamic of the place to shift. It had been an idyllic, peaceful, and harmonious environment; now the aggression and confusion of the outside world was contaminating it. The rest of the planet was beginning to discover what we had discovered years ago. The word was out, and it was clear to me that the party was coming to an end.

I looked out my front door one morning and saw a construction crew erecting a pier reaching out into the gulf, undoubtedly so visitors wouldn't have to wade in to shore like I'd done on my arrival. Surely they would never see the inside of that little Vietnamese rowboat, either. The pier was long enough to reach right out to a docked cruise ship.

Next were the roads. In my time there were none. We made our way around the island by either foot or long-tail boat. Now there were trucks pouring concrete in rippling ribbons up and over the hills around my home, creating streets that cars and buses and trucks would eventually move along, clouding up our pristine atmosphere with their noise and choking exhaust.

And then, of course, law enforcement showed up. The island had never had its own force; the locals handled any problems that arose among them, and if things ever got out of hand they would call in the navy to mediate any disputes. Now the army arrived, but all they did was bust the tourists and shake them down for money.

In short this was not the party I had RSVP'd for. It was beginning to feel like touring with the Grateful Dead had toward the end of my time with them: what had once been a free (spiritually speaking) and joyful dream was turning into a crowded, destructive nightmare. To escape I started spending more of my time at the north end of the island, where there was a beautiful temple dedicated to Kuan Yin, the Chinese goddess of mercy, the bodhisattva of compassion; her name translates to "one who sees and hears the cry from the human world." It was believed she sacrificed her own chance to reach nirvana, or heaven as it's called in the West, and instead vowed to remain upon the Earth until the last soul is liberated.

Koh Phangan was literally full of temples, and I'd visited most of them in the many years I'd been there, but this one was my favorite. It was located on a mountain road that led to a village called Chaloklum and overlooked Chaloklum Bay. If the weather was right, when standing outside the temple, I could see Koh Phangan's sister island, Ko Tao, some forty-three miles away.

However, it wasn't the view that drew me back again and again. It was the story of how the temple itself had come to be: A Thai woman who lived in Bangkok had a dream in which Kuan Yin told her to build a lighthouse on Koh Phangan, so the island's fishermen could see their way back after darkness fell. When she first came upon the site, she knew it was right because it was exactly as it had appeared in her dream. When people heard about what she aimed to do, many donated funds for the project; so much money came in that the woman (and a monk who advised her) decided to build a shrine to Kuan Yin instead of a lighthouse. The temple was ornate in style; its main building housed the traditional statue of Kuan Yin, and outside a big Buddha smiled out across the sea.

The temple became a landmark of the island, and Thai and Chinese people came at all hours to worship their goddess there. At night the temple's lights shone over the bay, guiding the fishermen home—so the woman's original dream was fulfilled after all.

This appealed to me on so many levels. As I sat in the temple day after day, watching the worshipers come and go, I thought of that one first woman who'd had the idea to build the place and how she had the courage to trust her intuition. Perhaps she had been just an average Jane before that—a housewife, a teacher, a businessperson, who knows? Then this dream totally derailed—in a good way—the direction in which she thought her life was going. All of a sudden she was a human with this divine connection, this mission to facilitate the enlightenment of total strangers.

I could relate to this. Not that I thought I was any sort of inspiration to anyone at that point, but I had already seen the effects of this kind of providence in my own life. I'd been a dissatisfied college student until I'd experienced a Grateful Dead show. I'd been a Dead Head until I'd gotten that call to caddy at the British Open in

Scotland, met Lance, and learned about Koh Phangan. Now I'd been living on this island for the better part of a decade, but nothing had intervened in that time. Maybe I was just supposed to be there for that long, or maybe I had stopped looking for signs because I was so comfortable where I was. If fate wanted me, I thought, it would come and get me. It knew where I lived.

As the construction and influx of tourists around the island continued unabated, I retreated more and more often to this temple, where I'd hang out with the monks and nuns who were there on retreats. They'd practice their meditation, and I would follow suit. With the low-hanging sun shining bright off the bay and a heat haze dropping down over the mountain, the silence and purity in that place some afternoons was radiant, a wave of peaceful energy rising up through the forest that surrounded us. It was intoxicating, this feeling of being so utterly in harmony with others, with the world; it drew me back again and again. I skipped parties to go practice meditation instead, to sit in that ancient silence and open myself to a world I hadn't known existed—a way of existing both within oneself and at one with the larger universe, separate from the many distractions and trappings of the modern world but deeply embedded in humanity itself.

In this state nothing else existed for me. The many fears and desires that had plagued my life were slowly beginning to lose their grip on the personality I had misinterpreted as my true self. The only thing I really wanted was to deepen this experience of emptiness. I had no idea where it was all heading, but that no longer seemed to matter, for I now began to trust the power of my own experience. I began to understand what detachment really is: not some passive, checked-out state of mind but a paradox wherein one is far removed from the many fixations of the ego. There were no possessions to hide behind, no sounds in the distance, not even the temple or the monks and the nuns. There was only darkness and silence except for the low hum of the universe, the essential om, the vibration of all things creating one lasting collective note. I felt so removed from the world as I had once known it, and at the same time I had never felt more present within my life.

Some nights when I left the temple, my soul was so light I felt as if I could float through the clouds and across the bay, back to my home beneath the lighthouse. The walk was long, but I always enjoyed it and used it as a time to decompress, to return to the world with more clarity and an awakened sense of wonder. I was just beginning to acknowledge the unfolding of my life and all the beauty that surrounded me.

One night as I was returning home, I was crossing an old coconut plantation—my usual route. Though some of the trees remained, and they still bore fruit, no farming had been done there in decades, from what I'd heard. Now an extended family of sea gypsies occupied the land—real kind and easygoing people I had grown to love during my time on the island. This night their home was dark; it was well past midnight, and most folks in the area were asleep…though not everyone, it seemed. I saw in the distance a burning kerosene lamp, its flickering yellow flame like a beacon on the horizon, like the temple woman's lighthouse guiding me toward the port.

I changed direction, and within a few minutes I saw the lantern belonged to a forest monk who had somehow found his way to Koh Phangan; most of them came from Issan, the northeast corner of Thailand. He sat next to a tiny hut—not his, as forest monks are nomads, never staying in one place for more than three nights—near the tree line of the rainforest, and around him in a semicircle were the elders from the gypsy family. As I approached they all recognized me and invited me to sit with them, which I did eagerly; although I had met many monks in Thailand, I had never met a forest monk and was so interested in hearing what he had to say. These guys were the real deal—they renounced worldly pursuits to devote themselves to spiritual work and kept alive the practices of the Buddha and his earliest disciples; they were known as meditation specialists, and their lives were much stricter and much more focused on the experiential value of meditation than those of temple monks, who mainly performed ceremonies and studied ancient scripture. Everyone in every class of society respects the forest monks, and it's considered a great honor to be able to give one of them food and water. Some even believed they had supernatural abilities. For sure they could see deeply into the heart of whomever or whatever they focused their energy upon.

As I took my place in the semicircle around the kerosene lamp, I thanked everyone quickly for allowing me to sit with them. They all nodded and smiled at me except for the monk, who stared at me as if he could see right into my brain or perhaps right through it. I cleared my throat and shifted my position, feeling a little uneasy and very vulnerable in front of him despite his slight stature and apparently young age. The power he projected, the aura of awareness that surrounded him, were insistent, commanding even.

He stayed that way for several minutes, just scanning me from inside out, and the family elders waited patiently in silence. Finally he spoke.

"You have no home."

I smiled nervously. "Ah, I do, here on the island." I raised my hand and sort of pointed in its direction of the lighthouse on the hill but then lowered it again quickly when he didn't follow.
He considered me in silence once more. "You are waiting for a sign."

Now I laughed. Just once, and only because his words were making me nervous, sending chills up my spine. Yes, they were general statements, the kind that any TV psychic threw out to the hopefuls in the audience, so vague that anyone could find something to relate to them. But when I really thought about it, he was right: I didn't have a home. Koh Phangan was where I dwelled at the moment, but I always knew that could (and most likely would) change at some point in time—when I got some sort of sign telling me that it was time.

I cleared my throat and drew a serious look over my face. "Yes," I told him. "Yes." It was all I could think of to say.

More silence. His dark eyes bore into me; I could see the flames of the lantern dancing in them. "You've found a meditative practice that works for you."

And with that, with just the thought of my meditation practices in the temple, my whole body relaxed. I let out a slow breath. "Yes," I said again. "I've been meditating with the monks and nuns on retreat at the Kuan Yin temple."

The forest monk nodded, the slow, knowing gesture of a sage despite his youth. "You're doing well. And these practices will deepen over time," he told me, his words slow and careful as if he were interpreting some divine message from a garbled text. "Your future teachers, however, will come in many unconventional forms. Just make sure you have your eyes and your heart open to receiving them."

I nodded, trying not to appear as overeager as I felt. "I will."

And that was all he had to say on the topic. After I made my promise, it seemed the case was closed, and his face softened. The corners of his mouth creased in a gentle smile, and he sat back, leaning on his hands on the ground behind him—a very casual pose for someone so revered. He and the elders returned to the conversation they'd been having before I had arrived, and they included me in it like I'd been sitting there all along. Thankfully my Thai was good enough that I could follow the conversation. Whereas I had assumed they'd been having a deep, philosophical discussion about matters of the soul and eternity, the talk revolved around more mundane subjects, such as how good the local mangosteen crops were that season and how the construction of the pier was going (everyone on the island had an opinion on that, most of them not good).

Then it turned to travel, and I was once again surprised that the forest monk had so much to say. He'd been all around Thailand but not much outside of that.

"You must be a traveler," one of the elders said to me. "Otherwise how could you have ended up here?"

Everyone had a good laugh at that then he implored me to tell them about the places I had been—the United States, Europe, just a handful of places, really, but they listened with rapt attention nonetheless. Except for the monk, all of these men had been born and bred right on the island; some of them had never left, not even once.

"So if you could go anywhere," I asked the group in return, "where would you like to go?"

The variety of answers surprised me. One just wanted to see the rest of Thailand; another thought it might be fun to see all the big cities of the world—just to visit, of course. He could never live in such a chaotic environment.

"I'd like to see the Himalayas," I said when the question came back around to me, and the forest monk sat right up.

"Me too," he said in a hushed voice. "I've been told there are many wandering siddhas that travel through the Himalayas, going for years without any human contact. Can you imagine such an existence? Completely hidden from the world for possibly your entire life?"

A siddha, in the Hindu philosophy, is a sage—a human being who, through meditation, has transcended his own ego and the confines of a conditioned mind and lives in full awareness of himself, the world around him, and the universe and its ways as well as where he and others fit into it. His physical body has changed too; in this enlightened state, it is dominated by sattva, meaning it is pure, uncontaminated, and spreads no disease or evil in the world. It's said that many of them occupy a secret land deep within the Himalayas called Shambala.

"Perhaps that is where you will find your teachers," the forest monk told me after explaining about these ethereal beings' hidden home. "One day, one day."

The comment was a throwaway, I thought—just something to say in conversation in a teasing or joking way. Sure, Forest Monk, I'll go find the mystery siddhas in the Himalayas, no problem. Let me get right on a plane and do that. I laughed a little when he said it, and so did he, affirming my belief that this was just lighthearted talk. It didn't mean anything.

But hours later, as dawn broke and I was finally continuing on my way back home, a revelation hit me so hard that my legs ceased to work. I stood in the middle of the coconut plantation field, the fronds of the scattering of palm trees that remained ruffling and shushing in the morning breeze. On the horizon a line of pink radiated up from the earth, fading into tangerine orange and then the lavender of the sky as it lightened. In the middle was just the rounded top of the sun, glowing like the forest monk's lantern in the night but a billion times brighter.

One day, one day.

Finally I had seen my sign. And deep down I knew that it was time to go.

THREE

Within a month I had sold my house and left Koh Phangan. Sailing away from the island on the same boat that had brought me there eight years earlier, I felt happy and sad at once: happy that I'd had the opportunity to see this place, to befriend its people, to experience what life was like in paradise, and sad, of course, that I was leaving it. However, I was also sad for the island itself, which truly had become commercialized and overrun by tourists. It was no longer the oasis it used to be, and I felt bad for the people who were native to the place, who had no choice but to remain there for the rest of their days. Watching the white-sand coastline recede as the boat carried me farther and farther out to sea, I sent up a little prayer for them to whatever gods were listening, hoping that the powers that be could keep them safe and, most important, bring them peace.

Back on the mainland I took some time to get acclimated to life again, to the hustle and bustle and the dirt and smog and the people, who seemed to have grown louder and coarser the longer I'd been away. And this was just in Thailand, which was nothing compared to the Western world. I hadn't been to New York in a couple of years; I could only imagine the culture shock I'd experience the next time I went back to caddy.

The other thing I did, of course, was buy an airline ticket to India. I wanted to get there as soon as I could, though I had no idea what I'd do once I did. As I handed over my money and got my slip of paper in return—my boarding pass for the plane—the words of the forest monk rang in my head: Your future teachers will come in many unconventional forms. Just make sure you have your eyes and your heart open to receiving them. I hoped that this was open enough, this jumping into a new life in a new place without even thinking of a safety net. I'd never been to India before, after all, and wasn't sure what to expect.

But then again, I told myself, I'd never been to Koh Phangan once either, and look how well that had turned out.

The plane ride was blessedly short—just under four hours until I set my foot on Indian soil for the first time. And no lie, for a moment I thought I had gotten off at the wrong stop and was caught up in a Grateful Dead caravan once again. New Delhi was just like the concerts used to be but on an enormous, universal scale: all the colors and the people and the scents and sounds… It was overwhelming, to say the least, and not always in a pleasant way. The first thing I smelled when I got off the plane was burning garbage, and I made my debut on the streets of New Delhi with the neck of my shirt pulled up over my nose.

Still, I could already tell this was an amazing place—again, though, not entirely a good amazing. India is a land of paradoxes and extremes, of excess and poverty, of profound beauty even in its degradation. Yes, the air was full of acrid smoke from the trash that had been set afire, but it also smelled of the fresh jasmine a young woman wove together and sold. She sat against a building, literally surrounded by a mountain of the blooms, piecing them together into necklaces and crowns to be worn or to be placed as offerings on altars of worship. The pollution in the city was stifling; a cloud of vehicle exhaust and diesel fumes seemed ever present in the atmosphere. But underneath that was a layer of incense, a rich, musky scent that came from nowhere and everywhere all at once.

In those first days I simply wandered around the city in a daze, drawn intrinsically from one thing to the next, just following wherever my eyes or ears or nose led me: To the vendors selling sweet-smoky curries on the side of the road. Toward the blaring horns of the trucks and rickshaws, their hulls painted vivid greens and yellows and reds. Toward the mosque that called its people to worship five times a day with the haunting and timeless adhan. Temple music was ubiquitous in the streets, playing from before dawn 'til far past dusk, far past midnight even. Perhaps it never ended. The shops, the bazaars, the little shacks that I soon discovered were actually restaurants—all of it was incredible to me. And terrifying. And I loved every minute of it.

India is home to more than a billion people, more than three hundred thousand of them packed into the 573 square miles of the capital city. And all of them, it seemed to me, were out on the streets at once. Like New York, this was a city—and a country—that never sleeps; at any hour of the day or night you could find people out shopping and bargaining and eating, pulling carts full of wares or just sitting on a curb, watching the world go by. Nothing was ever quiet in New Delhi; there was none of the Indian peacefulness and enlightenment I had imagined. At least none that was obvious to me at the time, though I'll admit I didn't know where or how to look. I thought I was heading down the right path, the one the forest monk back on Koh Phangan had set me on, but I was really just traveling in the same circle over and over again.

It wasn't until I truly opened my eyes to what was around

me that I began to understand: there was no meaning in this chaos, no peace. That was something I could only find inside myself—a remedial lesson, perhaps, but one I believe we all need reminding of now and again. My reminder came from the people of India, who are so open, so willing to share themselves with total strangers. They are not afraid to look each other in the eyes and right down into each other's souls. This is namaste—the silent acknowledgment that the god within me recognizes and bows to the god within you. When they looked at me in this way, it was if they were saying, "Go ahead. We have nothing to hide. You are welcomed. Come in and go as deep as you want."

I lived for those timeless moments, those little interactions that happened every day. They renewed me and my faith in humanity, in the connections we all have with one another, like we're spiders sitting along the sides of a very large web. When one of us moves, the others feel the ripple, and so we must be careful where we tread—another beginner's lesson we learn again and again in life.

Those moments also made me sad, though, and sorry for our world, our so-called civilization. We think we're advanced, but all we're doing is hiding behind walls and electronic devices and blocking ourselves off from what really matters: that connection, that web on which we live. We've become so preoccupied with what's next, with what's to come, that we've totally lost sight of what is. We don't see our inner gods in one another anymore; all we see are means to ends, and if you can't help me then what good are you? We have needs we think have to be met, though they have nothing to do with our spirits and souls. We have things. We don't need people.

We have Wi-Fi, but we've lost our connectivity to the present moment.

#

There's a great Buddhist saying: life and enlightenment are nothing more than the joyful participation in the sorrows of the world. India is a living, breathing example of this, and in traveling around the country, I saw the truth of it over and over again.

I saw an old peasant woman, her frail body scarred by brutal poverty in a country where corruption allows the rich to loot the poor. I felt the ache of loneliness in her heart, saw the quiet desperation in her eyes as she made her way through another day, somehow managing to survive the chaos.

I saw young girls racing by on their way to school, fresh jasmine in their hair, so full of innocence and joy. Everything was a wonder to their minds, which had not yet been poisoned by society, by intellect and reason and religion. They were poor but didn't know it—materially, anyway. They did not yet know they could separate themselves from the world, and so they were rich in spirit, in all that humanity ultimately seeks.

In another village I saw a baby boy, naked, bright, and overflowing with smiles. He looked deeply into my eyes, to my soul, and let me know he had been coming to this planet for far longer than I had. I saw an old man, his back bent from forced labor, his body sunburned from many years working in the blazing heat. Those who stood above him in rank and privilege had taken his body as theirs, had abused him in ways to which he could not say no, not if he wanted himself and his family to live. He was broken and scarred, but still there was plenty of fire in his eyes, and he showed it to the world. Life, with all its madness and cruelty, had managed to break his body, but his spirit somehow remained untouched.

I saw a woman lying in a gutter, a beggar too tired to beg.

She'd given up on everything except her own breath, though she patiently waited for that to end too—for her life to end, for the gods to take her home.

And even in the poorest places, the women dressed in every imaginable color and wore bangles that gleamed in the sun. They gathered by the village well with their copper pots, collecting water to nourish their families for the day. Life was hard and demanding here, but you would never know it once you saw the beauty and dignity in their ancient eyes.

It was in one of these places—a town called Ranikhet, in the northwest of India—that I finally found a little of the peace I sought. I loved New Delhi, but it was so noisy, and it had become too much after a while. In conversation someone had told me that I would have to go high into the Himalayas in order to find silence, so that was where I headed, and Ranikhet was the first stop. It was a seven-hour train ride from the city and after that a three-hour taxi ride up to the mountain town. Ranikhet in Hindi means "the queen's meadow"; little did I know I would soon be entering the meadow of another queen, one who has been worshipped within these mountains since the beginning of time.

Weaving along the winding roads, I saw the Himalayas for the first time, and needless to say I was breathless at the sight. The emerald-green terraces carved into the sides of the mountains reminded me of the landscape of Bali; large riverbeds and gorges sat dry now, since it was summer, but would soon fill up and overflow when monsoon season came.

The higher the taxi took me, the deeper the silence that enveloped me from all sides, and I swallowed it down like water, feeling immediately how much it nourished and rejuvenated me. I had missed this calmness, this stillness, and remembered the lighthouse temple back on Koh Phangan. I couldn't wait to get out of the car, to be on land again just so I could sit and meditate, to let the silence work in me and through me. To be one with the universe again, or at least as close as I was capable of becoming to it at the time.

When I did reach the village, I paid my driver, thanked him, and watched as he headed right back down the mountain. How could he, I wondered, make trip after trip here and never want to stay? I'd just arrived, and already I never wanted to leave. Ranikhet was an entirely different world from New Delhi, with a purity to the air that could not be found anywhere below. Pollution simply couldn't survive at this altitude, so the air remained in its original, natural, untainted state. There were people about but much fewer, and they moved at a slower pace: there was no hurry, no stress in their day-to-day lives. Though it was somewhat of a city as well—actually a cantonment, or a permanent military station maintained by the Indian army—it wasn't as large as New Delhi and nowhere near as loud or garish.

Though down below the summer sweltered, reaching as high as 120 degrees some days, due to Ranikhet's elevation, more than six thousand feet on average, the temperature was actually quite cool—another unexpected relief that I immediately enjoyed. This was, in fact, why the army had chosen to settle there way back in 1869: so soldiers and officers could retreat there in the hotter months. The government of India also used it for the same purpose while the country was still under British rule.

These days, though the military was still present, Ranikhet didn't feel like an army town. I'd see people in uniform, but there was no intimidation factor; they were just as friendly and engaging as any other people I met. As far as those other people, they fell under the same juxtaposition I'd seen in New Delhi: there were the wealthy and privileged, and then there were the beggars in the streets. The "untouchables" who in many ways reminded me of some of the caddies I'd had the privilege of working with. Most of them were minorities who society had already written off as worthless and irrelevant because of their skin color or the fact that they hadn't spent their lives aggressively pursuing wealth, or because they lacked proper education, though in fact many were far wiser and more refined than the people for whom they caddied. As usual I gravitated more toward the latter population, as I found them to be the most real, the most in touch with themselves and the world around them. It's been said that you never know who you are until you're tested, and if that's true then people such as these had to be the most self-aware individuals on the planet. What a way to gain enlightenment.

I had been in Ranikhet for about a week when I came across a man who fit this bill. He was sitting against a building holding a hat in his hand—upturned, hoping someone would toss a few coins into it. I did so and then asked if I could sit with him. He smiled and ushered me down onto the ground next to him, eyeing the bag of food I carried the entire way, though he was too polite to ask for some. He didn't have to. It was my lunch, and I'd purposely bought an extra serving with the intention of giving it away.

"What brings you to Ranikhet?" he asked as he took a packet of food from me, nodding his head in thanks.

I was feeling thankful, too, that he spoke English. And what he couldn't say, I could piece together with my burgeoning knowledge of the Hindi language.

But I wasn't exactly sure how to answer his question. "I'm looking for something," I said. "I don't know exactly what yet."
He already had a mouthful of chicken tikka, shoveled in with a piece of roti. He smiled and nodded again, and I waited patiently for him to eat before he could reply.

"You are not alone," he said at last. "Ranikhet is like a stopping point for those who are on a journey somewhere else."

"Is that right?" I asked, scooping up some chicken with my bread as well. "And where do most of those people end up?"

Again he could not speak for the food that filled his cheeks. Instead he raised a hand and pointed—out toward the Himalayas. I followed his finger and gazed for a while at the mountains. Before I'd come to India, they had been my destination, but I'd been taking my time getting there, hadn't I? What is that about? I wondered. What was holding me back from them, from the teachers the forest monk had hinted I might find there? Didn't I want to learn how to better myself and, thus, the world around me?

My eyes traced the mountains' peaks, as visible from a distance as the many beliefs and patterns we carry with us from life to life. Am I good enough? Am I in the right place? Is what I'm doing right? Or do I need to do more? Always questioning, always doubting ourselves.

My big question, of course, was always: where am I going? And that was in both a literal and a metaphorical sense. I'd been searching for something my whole life, and I had found pieces of it along the way. I'd found a community to which I belonged with my fellow Dead Heads. I'd found my connection to the spiritual and energetic undercurrents of the world on Koh Phangan. In India I'd found myself in other people and them in me.

But what would I find in the Himalayas? They were so big, so vast, so grand and mighty—so unlike anywhere I had ever been before. Perhaps that scared me on some level. Maybe that was what had slowed me down.

"Why do people go to the mountains?" I said to the beggar with whom I was sharing lunch. Maybe hearing other people's reasons would help me realize my own.

He wiped his mouth with his sleeve. "Some go just to climb," he said and leaned back against the wall once more. "Some go to see the sights." He looked at me. "But there are a few…like you, I think…who go for other reasons."

I smiled at him. Was it that obvious? "And those reasons are…?"

He put his dish down on his lap. "There is a legend that north of here, far up in the hills, there is an ancient temple made of stone. But it's not just a temple, you see. It's a doorway—an entrance to what we call the Forbidden Valleys. There are nine of them, with nine peaks, and on each peak is another temple. The bells that ring on their altars have echoed throughout the valleys long before man started to record time."

He paused for a moment as if he were listening to some faraway sound, looking out at the Himalayas, as I had been. "Each valley has its own path to be traveled, and anyone who visits them must fully commit to mastering them," he went on. "But that is not an easy thing to do. It takes time. It takes dedication. It takes reflection. And when you reach the end, that doesn't mean your journey is over. You will find a doorway there, yes, that will lead you to the universe buried within your heart. But it will also lead you to another valley, and another path, and another door."

"So you're saying there's no end to the process of self-discovery."

He turned his head to me and smiled. "You tell me. Is there?"

I smiled back, understanding this was a rhetorical question. Because what was I there for if not to find myself, to understand myself and the world a little more? I understood exactly what he meant: just when we think we know it all, that we've learned all we can and are ready to call ourselves masters, we find out just how much we don't know. We might think we've reached the end, but we're back at square one. This happens over and over in life. Just look at mine: I started college and dropped out. I went on the road with the Grateful Dead. I went to Thailand. Now I was in India. And each of these steps was the result of another door that had opened to me. All I'd had to do was be in the right place at the right time.

"And that's why other people go?" I asked.

The beggar nodded slowly. "They go for the experience. They go to find themselves. They go to understand their places in the universe."

When I did not reply—too lost in my thoughts—he took another bite of his chicken tikka and chewed it slowly.

"And how do they find these things?" I asked at last. Because these were the things I wanted for myself, and here they were being laid out before me, as if I could just reach out and take them. It couldn't be that easy; nothing ever was. But he made it sound so enticing.

However, now he shrugged. A simple gesture, as if I'd asked him whether he thought it was going to rain later. "That is for each man to discover on his own." Then he went back to eating, sopping up the leftover sauce with more roti.

I sat back, too, holding my barely eaten lunch in my hands. Miles away the snow-capped Himalayas glowed in the midday sun, a blinding white. Even from this far I had to squint in order to look at them. From Ranikhet the mountains looked foreboding, stark, but now I knew: in the middle of them were these Forbidden Valleys. I picture them all lush and green, strewn with wildflowers and possessing the magic of life itself.

"Does anyone live there? In the valleys, I mean?" I asked, my train of thought spilling out.

The beggar put his empty dish aside and laid his hands contentedly across his belly. "Yes, but these are some of the highest places in the world and the most remote. So it is an insular existence.

They live from the land and have no dependence on the outside world." He paused and then grinned. "Oh, and it's been said that this is where the Western game of golf originated." He looked at me, blinking. "Are you familiar with it?"

#

We set out for the stone temple the following morning, the beggar man and I. As soon as he'd said the word golf, I could no longer deny this was the way to go, that I was meant, for whatever reason, to visit these Forbidden Valleys. It was still dark out when we left, as he took me out of town and onto a dirt footpath that led into the Himalayas. A reverent silence enveloped the mountains, the only sounds our trudging footsteps on the damp dirt and an occasional bird squawking somewhere within the thick tree cover. The air was pure and clean and crisp, with a faint scent of burning wood; the temperature in the mountains always dropped at night, and in the morning it was necessary to light a fire to keep warm until the sun broke through the ever-present fog.

As we wove our way into the mountains, I began to see the green valleys the beggar had told me of before and surrounding them the terraces I'd spied on my ride into Ranikhet. These were small, though; he promised me there would be much larger areas to come. The landscape around us was already so diverse, so alive with plants and the occasional river that flowed from the mountains and carried the melted snow down into the valleys. I couldn't imagine anything grander out there, but I also couldn't wait to see it.

"That is Dunagiri off in the distance," my new friend told me, pausing to lean against a large boulder. I had no idea how old he was, but his body did look a little worse for wear—a factor of the life he lived, of not having a home or knowing where his next meal would come from. The gods provide, he had told me, as had so many others since I had first arrived in New Delhi. But that had to be a difficult theory to wrestle with when your joints ached and your stomach cramped from lack of food.

"It's a town," he went on as I grabbed a piece of rock beside him. "Well, it's six small villages, really. Many sages have set up their ashrams there—Garg Muni, Sukhdev Muni, the Pandavas of Mahabharata, they all took shelter in Dunagiri at one time or another."

We sat in silence for a while, gazing out upon the countless peaks and valleys. We were four hundred miles and a lifetime, it seemed, from New Delhi. I had left there only a week prior, and already I'd begun to forget what the city had been like. The temple music no longer rang in my ears; the combating scents of trash and incense no longer waged their wars for my nose.

"It all looks pretty innocent from up here," my guide said at last, startling me a little, especially to hear such a cynical statement coming from his mouth. "However, once you set foot on any path within these valleys, things begin to change rapidly."

He stopped again, looking at me from the corners of his eyes, the sides of his mouth turning up in a grin. "These mountains have a very special way of deconstructing and removing all of the many pretenses we attempt to carry through our lives, and in so doing they dismantle everything that stands between us and a direct experience of life."

I understood then that his statement had not been cynical at all but a warning: turn back now if you don't think you can commit; this journey is not for the faint of heart. I thought about it for a moment. Was I ready for whatever these mountains would want to throw at me? When the time came, would I be capable of delving deep into myself, into my very being, and seeing what was there?

Would I have enough guts to experience myself exactly as I was as opposed to how I wanted to be? And, more important, would I have the patience and compassion to accept and acknowledge the many imperfections of my own existence?

No doubt about it. I didn't even need to consider these questions. What had I come here for if not to learn about myself and find some secret to how I fit into this world, how we all made up the variety of human existence?

I stood up and brushed myself off. I had rested enough. "I'm ready when you are," I said, and at that my friend jumped up as well, looking almost sprightly compared to how he'd seemed back in town. Perhaps these mountains really were capable of changing people.

"There are many hidden passes and valleys out there," he went on as we walked, gesturing out past the cliff up which our trail wound. "Only the yogis and siddhas know where and how to find them. Each passage has a specific power that addresses a different aspect of one's being and, in doing so, removes a veil that has obscured who the traveler really is and what his life is really about."

"Hidden, huh?" I mused. It was enough to spark my curiosity, and I pictured these wandering sages, free of belongings and the trappings of self, exchanging greetings as they pass one another on these paths. "Does anyone live out there? Besides the sadhus, I mean."

The beggar man stopped again, clutching and leaning on his tall walking stick. He looked out over the valleys again, as if they mesmerized him just as much as they did me.

"Rumor has it," he began, "the villagers spot an old man from time to time, but no one knows who he is or where he comes from. He seems to spend most of his time beyond the pine trees, where the landscape slowly disappears into the clouds, and might be a sort of caretaker of the valleys." He paused, eyes narrowed as he thought.

"It's very possible that he walked in from Tibet many years ago, after the Chinese invaded. The border is only a hundred miles away from here."

He picked up his stick and got going again. We walked in single file as the dirt path had narrowed considerably as the elevation increased.

"Has anyone ever spoken to him?" I asked. "Tried to find out who he is and where he's from?"

The beggar shook his head. "All who inhabit these mountains respect him, but they also fear him because the level of reality he is in touch with is not something that most people can handle in their present states. If they can even comprehend that it exists. Approaching him would be like trying to go up to a raging fire: the heat might feel good from a distance, but the closer you get, the more dangerous it becomes."

I smiled. I loved this guy's analogies, and this seemed like an accurate one. From all I'd heard about the siddhas, they were the most unusual beings in that they didn't buy into the bullshit most of us perpetuate throughout our lives; they don't have time or even a use for the deceptions in which we cocoon ourselves in order to survive. There is no ambivalence between their words and their presence, for their lineage demands complete authenticity and an uncompromising nature that would be more than any normal human ego could possibly handle.

"Do you think I could find this man?" I asked, for a moment feeling just full of myself enough to think I could withstand such a meeting where others couldn't—a grandiosity I would have to lose if I wanted to undertake this journey.

"Hmm." The beggar man hummed for a moment as he thought then he stopped again and turned to me. "If it is meant to be," he said, putting particular emphasis on that first word, "he will find you. That's how it works up here. But let me warn you."

He actually held out a finger and almost wagged it at me.

"You would be very foolish to wander into those valleys alone. As far as I know, no one who has tried that has ever returned. They are called forbidden for a reason. There are no maps out here to guide you, and no one can even show you the way. I can tell you how to get to the beginning of the path, but then you must find your own way and rely on your own inner guidance." He poked me in the chest. "You do not need to find this siddha. You must trust your instincts and have the courage to follow what you know in your heart to be true."

I was invigorated and terrified all at once. Just the thought of being out in this wilderness alone, in the midst of these ancient, holy places, would be a challenge to my psyche, and I was eager to begin. This would be the ultimate journey of self-discovery, a means of finding myself in the place that basically invented the practice. I knew I had baggage; I could feel it dragging behind me with every step like a heavy anchor tied to my feet. I had done a decent job so far in my travels of shedding the layers I needed to, just enough to allow me to trust myself and others as I went along. But there were so many left. And it was the prospect of losing them that scared me the most.

"If you are foolish enough to go on," my friend started up again, "and you do happen to spot this siddha, don't let his appearance fool you. He looks like me—like a beggar—but most consider him a master. He is not a guru, nor is he interested in your adoration or attention. A true teacher will never demand or expect either of those from anyone. A true teacher will want only to see you standing on your own two feet, not leaning on anything and fully grounded within the truth of your own humanity."

I nodded, though he walked ahead of me and could not see it.

This I had known, too, that knowledge and devotion to one's unique truth is everything to these wandering siddhas. Many of them came out of a tantric tradition that believed all in life is a potential source of wisdom, a catalyst on which one can strike a match and ignite a deep awakening. Tantra is, technically, a collection of meditations and rituals that came out of India in the fifth century and can be found in the traditions of the Hindu and Buddhist religions. I say it's a collection because there is no one set system to the practice, no one way that each practitioner must perform it. Think about Christianity, particularly Catholicism's Sunday Mass or confessional: these are things that are done the same way every time to bring about the same results.

Tantra, on the other hand, cannot be described so definitively. It is more of a long path one follows, a journey on which you are constantly learning and becoming more open to life and aware of yourself through meditation and other practices such as yoga; the use of mudras (gestures); mantras (words and phrases); mandalas (an image of a square inside a circle, with a deity at each side of the square); yantras (diagrams of the universal forces); and identification with and worship of deities, particularly in the Hindu religion. More important, we learn through our daily interactions with others and through a willingness to be completely naked to the world in which we live. That is liberation. Heaven is not some far-off destination; it is waiting right here for all of us in the midst of the lives we are currently living.

This might sound like a fun trip, but it is not for the faint of heart: in this process we must bring all that we hold within ourselves, all our secrets and our shame, our guilt and our frustrations, into the light of our awareness; we must acknowledge it, understand it, and learn to let go of it. Only then can we become authentic human beings.

Nothing is denied along the way in this tradition; there is no aspect of oneself that can ever be ignored or left behind. This comes in part through tantra's dissolution of the divide between the spiritual and the mundane—in its assertion that divinity is transcendent, that there is nothing in this world that is not in some way divine. And we can enter the path from any point along the way, but don't let that fool you into thinking there are no rules here. The tantric tradition might seem sort of loose and wild to anyone who has not yet experienced it or who does not truly understand it, but it requires incredible discipline to both embrace and embody such a life. This is why so few people choose to take the path at all and why it as yet remains relatively unknown in the Western world.

#

By the time we reached the temple, the sun was coming up. We had hiked all day and throughout the night with only short stops to rest and to eat along the way. We had talked some but not too much, which was good because it gave me some time to think about what I was doing there. *If you are foolish enough to go on*, my guide had said earlier on in our trip, and those words had stuck with me. Was I being foolish? It was a possibility. I was, after all, following a beggar I had met on the side of the road up an isolated path into a sparsely populated area of the world's tallest mountain range. What could go wrong?

The temple was just like I had expected it to be: shaped like a small house with a chimney-like structure toward the back; made of rectangular, dark-gray stones; dim and cool inside when we went in to see if anyone was there. Finding no one except an ancient statue of Sarasvati, the goddess of wisdom, we returned outside and just stood there for a while, both of us watching the sun rising up into the sky, its rays illuminating the valleys and the verdant terraces below. A deep silence surrounded me, an emptiness that seemed tangible, as if it could contain everything I could possibly imagine.

"Congratulations," my guide said, coming closer to stand next to me. "You have made it to Shambala at last."

I just looked at him for a moment then my eyes drifted back out over the valleys. So this was it—Tibetan Buddhism's hidden kingdom, a pure land that is as much a spiritual construct as it is a physical place. And, as the forest monk back on Koh Phangan had told me, this was where I might find my teachers. I laughed a little, remembering it now. Teachers? There was no one there but us. Who was going to teach me—the rocks? The silent temple? I didn't even hear birds squawking in the trees any longer.

Beside me, the beggar gazed off into the distance.

I paused, and then I looked at him.

He smiled.

How could I not have seen it?

"You're…you're my first teacher, right?" I asked him, pointing a wavering finger in his direction.

He looked at the finger and then at my face, his eyebrows lowered. "Is that what you think?"

I nodded slowly. "Yes."

The beggar man shrugged. "Then I suppose I am." He turned around and headed for a nearby boulder, speaking as he went. "Tell me. Have I explained to you about the game?"

He sat down by the large rock and leaned back on it, closing his eyes as his spine straightened out. I did the same next to him and felt the same relief.

"Golf, you mean?" I asked, trying not to sound too overly eager. I'd been wanting to ask more about it but hadn't found the right time yet."

He opened his eyes and looked at me, his head still resting against the side of the boulder. "Yes, it is golf I mean. But we call it something else here. We call it the journey of life." He looked out over the edge of the hill on which we sat, sweeping his hand across the vista. "And this is where, it's said, the game originated—right here in the Forbidden Valleys, the valleys of the gods." He looked at me and nodded. "You see, the Divine Mother originally created this tiny island we now call Earth as a playground as well as a classroom for Her children—just one of Her many supreme creations, for there are literally billions of islands in the universe similar to the one upon which we now sit."

Now he raised his hand into the air, making the same grand, side-to-side gesture, this time indicating the sky. "They, as are we, are scattered throughout this vast sea of space. It is perhaps the height of man's arrogance to think this little planet is the only one out there that is a home to what we have come to call life."

He paused to take a drink of water from the bottle I had passed to him. The man had come all this way with nothing but the clothes on his back and the hole-ridden shoes on his feet—as always, I imagined, confident that the gods would provide for them. I suppose I was helping to fulfill that destiny in a way, as I had brought a backpack with me filled with water and supplies that we might need for the road.

"There is an ancient story," he continued, handing the bottle back to me with a grateful nod. "It has been passed on from generation to generation since before time began, and it is told to all those who make it this far up the mountain. Would you like to hear it?"

I smiled and wiped droplets of water from my lips with the back of my hand. "Yes, I would," I replied.

He nodded and went on. "Not too long after this planet was

created, many beings of high intelligence—beings of light, with no bodies—came here from other galaxies without a plan for what life is. The Divine Mother recognized that although these beings were very evolved, they still needed structure in order to continue their development. At the same time She knew it would be essential for them to maintain a certain amount of freedom in order to grow and have the capacity to surprise and delight Her. So, taking on their form, She appeared to these beings of light and told them to create a game that was metaphoric and enigmatic; they also had to create the grounds on which it could be played. The game had to be challenging, with obstacles to overcome. It had to be imaginative but also instructive in the directions one could take, and there couldn't be too many rules. The game would have to honor the uniqueness of all Her creations, She said, by allowing each to maintain its freedom of expression. It had to be divine adventure, so to speak, that would inspire and prepare the beings of light—and later human beings—for the journey that we all must ultimately undertake."

I pictured these beings occupying the valleys below, shimmering masses of light and color floating this way and that, chasing one another like children on a playground.

"The Mother was very clear and precise with Her directives," my guide went on. "For She knew this game would be not just a game but a universal story of initiation. She wanted Her children to develop naturally, with open minds and playful attitudes toward life, which was why Her guidelines were so specific: make the game simple, make it fun, and make it endlessly eternal."

"Sounds like golf," I said sort of absently. "Sometimes those games seem like they go on forever."

The beggar man laughed and went on. "In the beginning the beings of light created a game in which there were only nine holes, in honor of the nine guardians that the Divine Mother originally sent here to watch over the Earth. They were the original caretakers of this planet, willing servitors of humanity, highly developed souls who had spent lifetimes studying and serving on other planets. As a result of their training, they possessed a profound experiential understanding of the true nature of reality. Because of this, and because they were in the process of creating the game of life here, from which others could grow and learn, they were sometimes referred to as gods."

"What really is a god?" I asked.

"Ah." The beggar smiled at me. "A god is simply someone who knows more than you do."

"Fair enough," I said, smiling and even laughing as well. "Fair enough."

"Now, these gods," he went on, "in creating the game of life on Earth, convened in a council of nine. Each god was responsible for designing a different portion of the playground—one to each of the nine valleys. Each valley had to have its own unique vibration, an energy that would affect all who entered there in a particular way. Each valley had to represent an initiation, a rite of passage through which one could pass not without difficulty, but if he made it through, he would be wiser than he was when he had started out."

Again he held his hand out in front of him, slowly moving it along the path of the valleys. "So they sat down with a large piece of paper and drew nine mandalas as a blueprint for the playground. These mandalas were vast, replicating the routings and patterns of the many highways in the sky. The gods used the form of a spiral as the centerpiece of their creations—the same form we find in much of nature, from seashells and sunflowers right on up to distant galaxies. These spirals served as an energetic interface between dimensions. These were not merely symbolic creations, though, for within their intricate and labyrinthine patterns are many hidden pathways and passages as well as obstacles, all of which have the ability not only to dismantle the many illusions of life but to stimulate the deepest levels of one's being—and in doing so assist humanity to integrate the many dimensions of our minds, bodies, and spirits."

"Sounds a lot like a game of golf," I said. "Just a little more esoteric."

My guide smiled at me again, raising a finger to point at me. "You are exactly right. These were the original prototypes of what we call golf courses today. The gods chose this structure because it provides the vibrations that are necessary for the growth and development of all those who choose to move forward in the quest for a truer life here on Earth. The game was designed to bring us closer to our sacred origins and introduce us to our true selves by taking us through the many passages of initiation and the ten thousand experiences that accompany them. On this journey we can experience the highs and lows of existence, and we must confront all our assumptions about and approaches to life. The game brings up all our preconceived notions of reality and invites us to examine them in such a way that over time we can begin to clarify and expand upon our own visions of life."

His lecture—and I mean that in the most academic sense; he was, after all, my teacher—went on for a while more. As the sun moved up higher in the sky, and parts of the valleys below fell into cool shadow, he told me how the original golf courses had been designed to stimulate the left side of the brain, connecting us to a direct experience of reality, one that is not mediated through concepts. You could say they were forms of direct divine inspiration—much, much different from what the golf game had currently become. The game's modern designs, in both the literal and the figurative sense, have very little to do with mastery of ourselves and our spirits. Unfortunately they in many ways symbolize our cerebral ineptitude, our contempt for nature, and our confusion about life. They merely point out how lost we have become and how far we have strayed from our origins; they are very graphic representations of how disembodied and disconnected we have become from ourselves, from each other, and from our purpose here on Earth.

I thought about this a good deal as he spoke. It was very troubling to me to see my livelihood, as it were, in such a new and different light. In the original game, the beggar asserted, the Divine Mother wanted Her children to look at themselves as if they were each a ball, not the person striking the ball. In this sense we are the planet, we are each other, even though we are all spinning through life on very different trajectories. This was the purpose of the game: to show us that the journey of life here on Earth is all about the adventures of the ball, not the things or people who attempt to control the ball or make it move. Only the ball knows its own true nature and what it is capable of. In fact, as we play, we find that our intentions in life are the wind that moves the ball, so to speak, and there is much joy to be found in taking responsibility for where we land in life. This ancient game was never intended to be competitive, and it certainly has nothing to do with how many swings one takes at life.

When you play on a golf course today, you are also tapping in to the intentions of the architect, but if his or her designs are not in harmony with the original intended plan of the planet then you will find that upon completion of your round, you will be out of balance and confused, as if you were lost in a labyrinth. Many of today's modern courses are merely monuments to man's ignorance, arrogance, and greed—the bigger, the better; the more expensive and exclusive, the more desirable—and we are doing ourselves no favors by stepping out onto those cursed greens, putting ourselves in the pathways of the projections of the unenlightened.

"Now let us talk about the game play itself," my guide said at last, drawing me out of my negative thoughts. "There are nine valleys, as we know, and so there are nine holes, just as there are nine planets, and nine guardian gods and goddesses designed the game. Each hole represents another level of personal enlightenment and presents a unique koan or a riddle that is intended to shake up the many projections and perceptions we all possess regarding ourselves, each other, and this vast universe, about which we truly know very little. Each koan puts us on the path to mastery of whatever that particular hole wishes us to accomplish."

"Like what?" I asked. "What will I have to master?"

With a solemn face, the beggar man held up a hand to me. "That is for you to find out if you choose to enter the valleys yourself. That is not something I can tell you. Each person's experience is as unique and individual as his or her game of life; what I might find there might be different from what you see. There are some constant goals, of course, but how we reach them—well, that is up to each of us, and only us."

I liked the sound of that. Obviously I had never fit into any "normal" society that well; if I had, I wouldn't have spent most of my adult life so far wandering the world from one place to another, looking for something that I couldn't even name. If I had wanted to do what everyone else was doing, I would have finished college, gotten a nine-to-five job, settled down, and had some kids. Which is a great life if that's what you want and if you can pass the challenges that will get you there (such as earning a diploma, landing a job, finding someone to marry, and so on). But those were not the sort of obstacles I was looking for.

I wanted to be challenged deep down in my soul, to find what was in there, turn it around and around, and figure out what about it made it uniquely me. Then I wanted to let it go. Not so I could be someone else but as a means of becoming that much closer to the world. And I don't mean the world as most people know it, full of noise and artificial light, with machines that can do almost everything humans can do. I needed something simpler and truer, something I could find only by giving up everything else.

And I found it so ironic, so funny, that this was all going to begin with a game of golf.

"In the beginning," my guide went on, "there were only four clubs with which to play. Each symbolized a unique aspect of one's inner wisdom, for there is a tool to overcome every trap out there; the wisdom lies in knowing how to choose the right one. And there were no guides."

"No guides?" I jumped in, surprised by this information. "You mean…no caddies?" I couldn't imagine the game without us.

"That is correct. It is each being's job to carry his own tools. In doing so man learns to stand on his own two feet, to take full responsibility for his choices and actions. There is no one there to choose the club or make his decisions for him. He must look at the situation that surrounds him, call upon what he knows or seek out what he does not know, and make the most informed choice he can—the one he hopes will produce the most satisfying result. However…"

He grinned at me again. "The gods did take on apprentices, as someone had to learn how to play the game initially. They had to have the knowledge to pass on. These were the ancient rishis and rishikas, the first humans to walk and play upon these lands. They were the originators of what you now call caddies and had spent many lifetimes caddying for the gods on other planets. They were trained within the temples of Lemuria to understand the labyrinth of life here on Earth. It is said that each one of us comes to this planet to acquire skills to be more godlike, thus it has always been a great honor to carry the sacred sticks with which the game is played and to learn about the ball of life. That is what brings us closer to the gods."

Of course I liked the sound of that: caddying as a sacred

tradition, as a means to fulfill our purpose and bring us further toward the state wherein we and the gods are one. And I'd long known there's more to caddying than just carrying around a bag of golf clubs. Caddies give insights and advice to players not only about the course and what clubs to use but also about the lives the players are attempting to live. There are so many facets to caddying, and each caddy is as unique as is the blueprint of his or her soul.

Sometimes, too, I had found that a caddy can act as a confidant. More than once a player has decided to spill some secret to me: how he wasn't happy in his marriage, how much money he made or owed, or that he really didn't like the life he was currently living and the person he had become.

I suppose, if I think about it, I did find something spiritual about caddying. It allowed me to be not the person who moved the ball but the one who tried to help the ball move in the best way possible. I had to, as my guide here had said, take in everything about my surroundings; I had to be aware of the challenges and obstacles of the course, draw on what I knew to devise the best strategy to overcome them, and give the player the best advice I could. It was a positive experience for me, a means of connection between me and nature and the person for whom I caddied. And any negativity on the players' part, or my part for that matter, just seemed to drag it down and obscure any relative information I was able to tap in to in the moment. In my most enjoyable rounds, I walked with people who were honest, open, and humble. And it always amazed me what would come through in those situations. The barriers and veils of the personality would no longer get in the way, and as a result we would both enter into a unified field—one that was filled with clarity.

"The training here on Earth is much different," the beggar went on. "Here it is not so much about learning the game. It is more about learning what it means to be human. The game, at least as we play it, was designed to teach us this over time—that it's not all about the life you think you should be living or the many realities you can imagine for yourself and others. What you are is what you are in this moment. Power, joy, and the magic of existence come from within, yes, but they also come from letting go of the daydreams and facing the life you already have. Only by embracing your own humanity can you fully realize the path to divinity." He paused as if in thought.

"This has always been a game of logic, a game for scholars. Which makes your Masters Tournament an apt name, yes?"

That gave us both a good laugh, and I had to agree with the statement.

"Yes, there was a time when being able to play this game," he went on, "did qualify one as a master of life. Unfortunately nowadays our obsessions and addictions have become the game of life we play, and I'm afraid mankind has mastered those far too well. We have definitely lost something along the way."

He turned his face to me. "But you. You are ready to find what we have lost?"

I looked at him, too, a firm, strong gaze. "Yes. I am ready," I said. But I had never felt so sure and so scared at the same time in my life.

He nodded once and then stood up. While brushing himself off and shaking the stiffness out of his legs, he continued to speak. "Each of the nine valleys out there has its own specific vibration, as I have already mentioned. But each also radiates its own color, creates its own distinct sounds, and carries its own unique fragrance. The farther you go into these hidden valleys, the more subtle the vibrations will become and the more sensitive and intuitive you must be in order to advance. You must match those valleys energetically not only through your understanding of yourself but, more important, through your actions and your embodiment of life itself. Do you understand?"

I nodded as I stood up as well. The sun was at about forty-five degrees overhead; it was midmorning already, but it still felt cold. I went to get a long-sleeve shirt out of my pack. "It means I can't force my way into the valleys, particularly the later ones. I have to approach them with…with a sense of respect."

"Yes, you do," my guide agreed. "The gods, unlike most everything else in your life, cannot be bribed or overpowered. It is only through sacrifice and service that we ultimately earn our way into the Promised Land." He stood at the edge of the hill, the drop-off at his feet, looking down. "It also means that everything you know and have experienced up until this point is no longer relevant. Your will to survive, your desire for more of the things that run your life—none of that means anything once you step out onto the course. These forces have brought you here in one way or another. But this is where their journey ends. From this point onward you will find yourself slowly letting go of what is known and surrendering to the unknown. There is nothing to manipulate or dominate out here and nothing to manipulate or dominate you. There is nothing to be gained."

He turned to face me. He raised his arm and pointed toward the distance behind me. "Go that way, and you will find the first tee."

It took me a moment to process what he had said. I turned halfway around and saw a rough pathway leading toward the downward slope of the hill.

"Wait," I replied. "You mean…you're not coming with me?" On the way up to this temple, I had been scared of being alone with him in the middle of nowhere; now I was terrified that he was going to leave me out there by myself.

"That is correct," he said and took a step back toward the dirt trail we had followed on the way up. "It is your own unique aspiration for a deeper, truer life that brings you up the mountain and on to the first tee—what the rishis and rishikas called the Altar of Life." He put his hands together in front of his chest and bowed his head quickly. "I wish you much luck, my friend."

He gave me one last smile and a bit of a wave, and with a few more steps he had disappeared on the pathway back into the trees, leaving me completely alone in the Himalayas.

FOUR

The pathway to the Altar of Life was lined on both sides by a thick, deep forest. The boughs of the trees overhung the road, creating a canopy of leaves that effectively blocked out the light, making the air even colder than it had been while I was in the sun. Still, I was surrounded by the fertility of nature, unobstructed by man's obsession with so-called development; everything was green and brown and fresh, everything lush and alive. I took in a deep breath, and the heady, musky scent of the wet earth grounded me, alleviating my worries and reminding me I had nothing to fear out here—not even the monkeys and leopards I could hear from time to time swinging and skulking through the forest.

The walk went on for several miles, giving me plenty of time to think, and naturally, given the conversation I'd just had with the beggar man, my thoughts turned to golf. As a caddy I must have walked hundreds, probably thousands, of miles already, up and down hills, across greens—much like I would be doing here, except now I thankfully would not have to carry the bags and burdens of others.

I remembered some of the golfers I had caddied for, most of them very wealthy and very lost within their own egos. Many of them spent their time either obsessing about some new material object they didn't yet have—like a new club, a new car, or another house—or bitching about some mundane aspect of their lives, such as how their last meal hadn't been cooked to perfection. That was all that mattered. Not how much they had improved since they'd started playing, not the friends they were playing with, certainly not their lowly caddies, whose advice they almost never took. Many would ask their caddies for opinions just so that when things didn't go as planned, they would have someone to blame. Their walks upon the golf course were merely parades for their own egos.

Then I remembered one guy who had been so different. He'd been friendly and open from the start and really eager to hear what I had to say not just about golf but about things going on in the world and whatever else I felt like talking about. The most memorable thing he told me was his idea that every golfer should keep two scorecards—one for his score and the other on which to record whatever memorable experiences he had at each hole. For example, "Hole 1: beautiful, warm spring breeze came in out of nowhere. Hole 2: spotted a yellow-beak finch in a nearby tree."

This guy really got it. I wondered what he was doing just then, while I was out there on that mountain trying to find myself. Hopefully something similar wherever he was. I was sure he would have enjoyed it.

My first few hours on the path were magical. I found a sense of contentment in the solitude that seemed to erase so many years of doubt and despair. I was beginning to feel as if I was finally where I truly belonged and at same time laughed at the paradox of not even knowing where I was or where the path was leading me.

As I continued to walk, I looked for signs of life but found none except the animals that accompanied me hidden in the trees. There were no humans, but there were signs that some had been there, at least, at some point: there were small shrines along the way, one every hour or so—places of worship that had been there for generations. They were situated usually at the base of a tree wrapped in colorful cloth and looked like little stone houses, not quite as big as the temple the beggar had taken me to but similar in function and similarly unoccupied. Not even a footprint to let me know someone else had passed that way in a recent time.

Then finally I saw a clue. About four hours into my hike, I came upon a tiny shrine that looked like it had been used as a hut. A trident leaned on the cloth-covered tree, a sign of honor to the Hindu god Shiva. To the side was a fire ring, a small circle of stones in which a smatter of embers still glowed faintly.

"Hello?" I called out, but no answer came. I waited, looking for somebody in the trees. But there was no one. The sun had passed its midday position by then, and I had to keep going, but it felt wrong somehow just to walk away. So, in respect, I did the same gesture the beggar had done as he'd parted from me: I clasped my hands in front of my chest, bowed my head, and said a vague and surprising little prayer for the person who had stayed there.

I'd never been a praying man, and I wouldn't say this rambling, silent monologue completely fit the bill, but it was a hope put out into the universe for that person's wellbeing, and that had to count for something. As I walked away I pondered why I'd done this; it had just seemed like the right thing to do. This place might have been empty, but it was steeped in the prayers and intentions of all who had come there before me. So I guessed I was just following suit.

#

As the afternoon wound down, I began to wonder if I was lost. I was still following the trail my guide had pointed out to me, and I hadn't seen any forks or branches where I could have turned off. Most of the way had been downhill, but now it had seemed to level off, so I figured I had reached the bottom. But I saw no temple, nothing that resembled any kind of first tee. The forest had thinned a bit, and through it I could see the horizon. The valleys out there just didn't seem to be getting any closer.

What am I doing? I asked myself, for the first time feeling a little bit of doubt that maybe I shouldn't have started on this journey after all. Maybe I wasn't as ready as I'd thought I was. I was also not real certain about my sanity at this point or the decisions I had made to get me to this point in my life.

"If I hadn't gone to Scotland…" I muttered to myself as I walked in what I was sure was another dead-end circle. But it was only my frustration and desperation talking, and I knew it. Up until that point I had been quite happy with the hand that karma had dealt me. Now I couldn't let a little obstacle throw me off the path.

I decided to sit down for a few minutes, to rest my body and try to get my bearings. Leaning back against the trunk of a massive, ancient tree, I closed my eyes and breathed deeply, grateful for this momentary respite. My feet hurt, my back ached, and I just wanted to be somewhere already. It wouldn't be long before the sun began to set behind the mountains that surrounded me, and for as beautiful as this place was, I was wary of getting stuck out there in the dark alone.

But it's the journey, I reminded myself silently, trying to get my mind into a meditative state. Not the destination. That was what I had always believed—quite the opposite of what passes for life today. People now seem to see only the things that they want to get; they are too focused on the prize and don't enjoy the game through which life is played. I'd seen it in golfers whose only concern was their scores. And, unfortunately, now I was seeing it in myself.

But I did my best to draw those thoughts back in, to confront them and dismiss them as the useless things they were. Once I felt more at peace, I opened my eyes again, and it was as if I had never seen the forest before. The green leaves and mosses seemed electric; the browns of the trees' bark were so deep, like an abyss into which I could jump. The silence was so complete I heard my ears ring in the absence of any other noise.

Without thinking, I reclined my body until I lay down on the ground. The trees' branches and leaves meshed together far overhead, the sun's fading rays beaming through the openings between. Everything swayed in a gentle breeze, like the Divine Mother was rocking me to sleep.

"What was I ever afraid of?" I asked aloud, keeping my voice to a whisper though there was no one to hear. I could never get stuck out here. And if I was lost, so what? There were worse places in the world to lose one's way. In a flash I realized I would rather die out there at that very moment, surrounded by all the Mother's holy creation, wandering around in search of something meaningful, than to return to so-called civilization and spend my remaining years stumbling around a life in which I'd never really believed.

Besides, I was too far in now to turn back. Wherever I was headed, I had to be closer to it than I was to where the beggar had left me. He'd said it was nine miles to the first hole; I had to be closing in on it. At least that was what I hoped. I could have been very, very wrong and been going the completely wrong way.

What a terrifying realization. But it was also very liberating, as I now stood completely outside the world of man. There was no one here to give me directions; every choice I made had to be my own, based only on intuition. Make or break, it was up to me, and I had no idea which would happen first.

I stood up and brushed myself off then got back on the dirt path. I would continue on and take my chances on the unknown.

As the sun began to set, finally I saw something: a spiral of smoke rising into the sky not far ahead. I hurried toward it, eager to catch whoever might still be there, hoping that person might be able to tell me where I was. When I got to the source, I found it was a tiny hut—just a one-room shack—set up on the ledge of a hill. I called out hello and waited for an answer. There was none. I went to the hut and knocked on the door. Again no reply.

But the wispy, white smoke still streamed out of the crack above the little hut's door, which meant the fire was alive. These weren't remnants, as I'd found at a shrine earlier in the day. Someone was tending these flames. Whoever it was couldn't have gone far, but another scan of the area around the hut showed no one.

I stood by the door, hugging myself and rubbing my upper arms; it was cold and getting colder as darkness came on. All I could think about was that fire and how warm it would feel on my fingers and toes. Finally I made a decision.

Reaching out, I pushed open the door slowly.

"Hello?" I said again as it swung back on its rusty hinges. "Hello?"

No one was there. And if there were no occupants then no one would mind if I went inside. That was my reasoning anyway. I tentatively set a foot into the hut, looking from side to side just in case. Everyone I had met in this part of the world had been nothing but friendly and generous, but what if this was the home of a crazy ax murderer living out in the woods? I doubted this would be the case; the hut was probably just the temporary home of an old monk or a siddha who had wandered off for some water.

When no one jumped out at me, I quickly brought the rest of my body inside and as soon as I did, I felt at home. As if I had stepped back in time, into an ancient world that I had known long ago. The room around me was primitive but seemed far more spacious than it really was, in part due to its spiral-shaped ceiling, which was covered in a layer of black from years' worth of accumulated smoke. It looked like tar, like lava ready to drip and ooze down to the floor. The whole place seemed alive, as sacred as any I had ever visited. The air was charged with such a powerful vibration it literally took my breath away.

The walls inside the hut were covered with pictures of the many Hindu goddesses and forms of the Divine Mother. The dirt floor had been swept of dust, and in the center was the fire, burning brightly off of one hollowed log. Shedding my pack, I sat cross-legged in front of it, holding out my hands to warm them. I closed my eyes, thinking I'd never felt anything quite so good as that warmth felt now. It didn't take long for it to combine with my exhaustion and lack of nourishment, and soon I was lying on the floor, fast asleep. Then the occupant of the hut came in.

I sat up quickly then got to my feet. "Uh, sorry." It was all I could think of to say.

But the man said nothing to me in return. He looked me in the eyes with a fierce but warm intensity that put me immediately at ease. He didn't seem surprised that I was there; in fact it seemed as if he had known I was coming and indeed that I was someone he had known for a long, long time.

As I puzzled over this, he continued about his business. He was an old man, his clothes little more than rags, with the tough, weathered look of someone who spent much of his life outdoors. His long, dark hair, which was beginning to yield to the silver and gray shades that usher in the last chapter of one's life, was wrapped up in a topknot. His face was a road map of wrinkles, as were the backs of his hands. But despite these markings of age, he had an eerie glow about him, as if his dark skin gave off an aura that shone out of his every pore, a light that reflected dimensions I could only describe as otherworldly.

He moved around the hut—putting down the pail of water he carried, stoking the fire—and it seemed as if he glided on air. Every movement was fluid, graceful, and it was obvious he was plugged in to something I knew very little about. His lightness was ethereal, but at the same time I could feel how grounded he was and his deep connection to the Earth. As I studied his features and attempted to figure out where he came from, it became clear that although he appeared Tibetan, no nationality or region could claim his soul, for he had no sense of individuality or self-importance. He was in the world but certainly not of it, at least not in the conventional sense.

Finally he did turn to me and gestured with his hand for me to sit back down. I obeyed, and he took a seat next to me before the fire. Beside him he laid down a small bag that contained his few worldly possessions, and from it he pulled a chillum. I watched as he mixed together a blend of tobacco and hashish, his every movement a prayer charged with life force, respect, and a deep devotion. I got the sense that there was nothing in the world to which he was not connected. He moved his hands in elaborate spirals, but the designs came naturally because they were from within, reflections of the life he had lived and the many paths upon which he had already traveled.

Once he'd prepared the chillum, he paused for quite some time, now filling the room with his intentions and prayers. Then he reached into the fire with metal tongs and pulled out a burning ember, which he placed on top of the chillum. He raised the chillum to his third eye, offering up what he had just created, and took a huge puff. He exhaled the smoke up into the spiral ceiling, feeding the black lava with some more life force.

As the smoke settled, he handed me the chillum, and though I hadn't smoked in years, this was too sacred to pass up. I carefully took my first puff, and the tobacco was so strong I coughed up most of what I had taken in. The old man laughed. I tried again, this time inhaling only a fraction of the smoke in the chillum. Immediately I felt relaxation radiating through my body, like a raindrop had hit the top of my head and the ripples were gently spreading down. I felt my body open in a way I'd never experienced before, and I could sense the prayers and mantras that had been recited in this hut over time; I felt ancient energies vibrating up through the earth and into me, going right up my spine. The many plates of armor I had fastened to my body over the years of my life, all the masks and defenses I had worn and built, began to melt and give way. I bid them good-bye even if it turned out to be for only a moment. This was the openness I had been searching for: this liberation, this freeing of the energy I had previously invested into protecting and defending who I thought I was.

But of course I found it terrifying. The magnitude of the moment, of being so exposed to myself, was more than I could handle, and I felt myself trying to retain my grip on the past, pulling back, retreating from the abyss that threatened to swallow me whole. I was afraid of death as I never had been before, but at the same time I was aware of the irony: I'd spent so long looking for this awareness, and now that it was in front of me, I was unable and unwilling to enter into it.

As I pulled myself back from the threshold of this expansion, my body reacted. I felt dizzy; I started sweating. Finally I jumped up and ran outside, where I vomited on the ground and then stood with my hands on my knees, waiting for the nausea to subside. As it did, I could feel myself returning to my body little by little: hands and arms, legs and feet, head and mind. I took great lungfuls of the cold evening air, letting it fill me up, then released it out as slowly as I could.

Back in the hut the old man smiled and nodded at me, silently acknowledging what I had just experienced. I went and joined him by the fire.

"Is this where you live?" I asked him, and he nodded. I thought for a moment that he didn't speak—maybe a vow of silence, or maybe it had just been so long since he had that his throat had somehow lost the capacity.

But in that I was very wrong. The old man had a lot to say. He told me all about his life and how he spent his time going from one temple to another all over the mountains, keeping the fires in them burning. This was one such place.

"Also people come to me when they are searching for something," he said, his voice scratchy with age, and I shifted a little uncomfortably. Did he already know why I was there even though I wasn't exactly sure myself?

If so, he didn't let on. He simply went on talking about others who had found their way to him there in the woods. Once two old women came to his hut, each harboring a deep sadness from the difficult things that had happened to them in their lives. They sat with him for a long while, smoking as we had just done and telling him everything that weighed heavy on their hearts.

"Soon that sadness rose up out of them," he said now in his gentle voice, gesturing toward the blackened ceiling. "And it remains here. They no longer carry those burdens with them."

Another time a young man came with profound unhappiness about his life. He sought the old man's wisdom and help then returned the favor by offering him ghee to cook with. The old man took it but later threw it into the fire, for he already had some and said there was no need to horde or store anything.

"The Divine Mother provides all I need," he told me. "She gives me what I need every day."

As his soothing, gentle voice droned on, the warmth of the fire made me feel at home, as did the Divine Mother's watchful gaze peering out at us from the pictures all around the hut. You are in the right place, her eyes told me. And your journey is just beginning.

I smiled. How could this primitive hut give me more comfort than I'd ever found in any hotel? It was a mystery, as was this old man who continued talking soothingly to me as I fell asleep, my pack under my head as a pillow, my body relaxed into a deeper place within the universe than I had ever imagined.

FIVE

With the dawn of the new day came a thick fog that worked its way from the high Himalayas down into the valleys. The breath of the gods was just giving way to the first rays of sunlight when I opened my eyes, and I looked around the dim room for the old man. He was gone; I was alone. I wondered if I would ever see him again.

I didn't have to wait too long for an answer, though. Grabbing my pack, I headed out of the hut. Standing on the edge of the ledge where the hut sat, I saw the old man a distance away, standing atop a huge boulder, stretching his arms—his whole body, really—up toward the sky, opening himself to a new day. I just stood and watched him for a while, so moved by this timeless image, drawn in by the vortex of energy he was creating with his body and the sacredness of the space throughout the valleys. Finally our eyes met, and he smiled gently, giving me tacit permission to go over to where he was. I sat down on a rock close by and watched him finish up his morning ritual. The peace I had long been seeking seemed to stream out of his body in the same way the morning light now filtered through the clouds. Eventually the old man settled into a sitting pose with such grace and balance it was like watching a snowflake fall out of the sky and land upon the earth.

We both sat there in silence for what seemed like an eternity. Then finally he spoke.

"You are required to make only one offering in these

mountains, and that offering is your self with all of its complexities, with all its paradoxes and all its untapped potential. All of the many things in life we so desperately hang on to ultimately must go if we are to continue on and make our way into the valley of the gods."

I nodded my head. This much I had known: that I could not begin this journey—much less finish it—with all my archaic issues still in place. At the very least I had to be willing to give up those things I'd been holding on to for so long—my ego, my sense of safety, my myopic view of the world, all the predispositions I didn't even consciously know I had—as the journey went along. Could I do it? Was I willing?

"I am ready," I said.

The old man stood up, and I followed suit. Then I followed him onto another dirt path, this one to bring us to the stone temple at the top of the hill. Halfway up we stopped in the shade of a strange, old evergreen tree. It was enormous; it had to be two hundred feet high, with needles the length of my arm. Bright-blue berries clung to the branches and littered the ground around the trunk, where they split open and spilled their seeds.

The old man bent down and scooped up a handful of the seeds. He tossed them in his palm for a moment, testing their weight and shaking off the dirt. Then he handed them to me. They were small and round, reddish in color, with a hard outer shell.

"These are called rudraksha seeds," he said. "They are also called the seeds of compassion, for many people within these mountains believe they are formed from the tears of Shiva and are possessed of shakti, the goddess's feminine energy."

I nodded again, listening to the lesson of my second teacher.

"You'll find them all throughout the Himalayan valleys, where the yogis have used them for centuries as prayer beads and strung together as malas. They are used for meditation and healing and to refine one's senses and usher in a state of tranquility. Seekers have used these seeds for thousands of years to cultivate physical, mental, and spiritual wellbeing on their paths to enlightenment and liberation."

These seeds were not completely unfamiliar to me. I had seen people wearing them around their necks in New Delhi and had learned they help neutralize negativity and accelerate one's development.

I looked down at them in my hand, at all the ridges and crevices of their outer shells. They looked like the old man's face, a road map of wrinkles, each leading to a life experience, to a lesson learned.

"Some believe that these seeds hold the secrets of evolution and creation within them," the old man continued. "And that may very well be true. They are in many ways amulets that bestow power and protection on all who possess them. However, long, long ago they had a much different purpose. You see those plateaus and labyrinths off in the distance?"

He raised his weathered hand and pointed out over the hills and valleys.

"Those were once golf courses," he went on. "The ones the rishis and rishikas created. And when they played, they used rudraksha seeds as their golf balls."

An image formed in my mind of nine ethereal beings, little more than mist and light, projecting these seeds high up into the air and deep into the valleys. A primitive golf game indeed but one so unburdened, so joyful, it was difficult to compare it to the modern golf I knew.

Still, I couldn't imagine how these small seeds could travel more than a few yards. "But they're so light," I said, rattling them in my palm, demonstrating how easily they rolled about, clicking and clattering off one another.

The old man smiled. "You are correct. These seeds are at the mercy of the wind once they are launched into the air."

Nothing like the modern game of golf, I thought, where every stroke was calculated and exact, designed for one purpose: to get the ball directly in the hole. I imagined the chaos that would ensue if the ball could be thrown off course by any gentle breeze.

"So how did anyone win?" I asked.

The old man shook his head. "You miss the point. When a seed was launched into the air, it was at the mercy of the wind. It could not get to its destination without that driving force to move it. In much the same way, the power we seek and even rely on comes not from our egos but from our ability to navigate that wind, to ride the waves of life as they come, and, more important, to understand the forces that go into creating them. This was the intent of the original game. It was not about power and domination. There were no winners or losers."

Just the thought of this left me speechless. With no winners and losers, the modern golf industry would implode. Every aspect of the game today is somehow geared toward power and domination. From the balls and clubs we use to the devices to measure distances and even to the shoes on our feet, everything is factored in to this winning equation. If we have the "right" brand or the "right" gadget, we believe, we will come out on top. And if we don't, well, there's probably something we can buy to help us next time.

This, of course, is a fallacy, one we have constructed around ourselves over time. There is no magic gadget we can use to make us into winners. Just look at all the technological advances in golf in the last few years and the increased physical and psychological conditioning that is expected of its players. Today professional golfers can hit drives fifty yards farther than their predecessors could thirty years ago, but, interestingly, their scores more or less remain the same.

Not even the newest, most cutting-edge technology could ever make us masters of anything; instead it expresses our ineptitude and our confusion about where our real sense of power lies. Instead of realizing that it lives within ourselves, we give it away, investing it in devices or other people or whatever we think will help us get ahead in life. This just reinforces the illusion that mastery is based upon acquisition. We've erected this barricade, this distance, between us and our purpose here on Earth, and the chasm grows bigger every year.

"Are you eager to begin the game?" the old man asked me, leaning close to me, a bit of a twinkle in his eyes.

I laughed. "Yes! I'm ready." Now that I'd been thinking about golf, as problematic as it was, I'd become anxious to get out into the valleys and see what the original course was like.

In response the old man beckoned me forward, and again we set out on the dirt path, each with a handful of rudraksha seeds.

SIX

"Within each hole," the old man told me as we hiked up the hill, "there is an ancient story waiting to be told. Modern man is only in the early stages of tapping in to these stories. These valleys and the holes they represent are very demanding, as is the terrain you are now about to ascend. There will be dramatic shifts in altitude and a scarcity of oxygen, which is why the ego will soon be left grasping for all it is about to leave behind. When you enter a valley, you must learn to surrender the many conditioned parts of yourself. Only then will you be able to proceed to the next hole."

"That shouldn't be too hard," I said, as it seemed like a natural process, one that wasn't based on aggression.

"We will see," he said, and we continued on the rest of the way in silence. The climb didn't seem to take nearly as long as my other hikes so far had, and I was grateful for this. When we arrived at the ruins of an ancient Shakti temple at the top, I felt refreshed rather than tired, renewed rather than lost and confused. It was a nice change of pace.

Just past the temple was a very small plateau that looked out onto the countryside below, revealing a beautiful vista of fertile rice fields, lush valleys, and flowing rivers, all framed by the snowcaps of the Himalayas in the background.

The old man came to stand beside me. "This is where it all begins," he said with a big, bright smile and a twinkle in his eyes. Then he looked down at my feet. "Take off your shoes. You are now on sacred ground, and in order to proceed you must maintain a connection with the earth. You must be fully grounded within your body in order to progress."

I did as he said. The ground was cool and soft beneath my feet, and I dug my toes into it. If I had to be grounded, might as well go all the way.

"The first hole," the old man went on, "is known as the Valley of Hope. This is where the true consecration begins for you. This is where you enter the valley of the gods. People have come to this very spot for centuries in order to refocus their lives, to swing out at what they hope and dream for."

He paused and looked at me, his face growing solemn.

"In order to make this journey," he continued in a low voice, "you must leave everything behind. All of the many affectations you attempt to hide behind, whether they're spiritual or material, will no longer be of any use to you once that first drive is launched. You must surrender this part of yourself and accept that it will never return. Out here you are naked and alone with yourself. You will be stripped clean and exposed to your own deepest hopes and fears."

He gestured out over the valleys. "This wide panorama you see will seduce your intellect and touch your heart in a very direct way, offering you the opportunity to expand beyond the confines of your own present conditioning."

He put an arm around my shoulders and moved me a quarter turn to the left. "This open field over here is a practice area—a staging ground of sorts. This is where the rishis first taught their kriyas and breathing exercises to the uninitiated. The breath gives birth to form, and the kriyas open the student up, beginning the process of untying the many karmic knots that are wrapped around the nadis, the channels where consciousness flows throughout our bodies. In order to fully experience life, these channels must be open so the cosmic streams of energy can freely flow through us."

This I was familiar with. Kriyas, in yogic terms, are movements that awaken and release the flow of kundalini, which is the creative force that lies dormant within the human form. So the rishis, it seemed, had created these movements and breathing techniques to facilitate and support the opening of the many streams of energy that flow throughout the body and connect all of us to this vast universe, the mandala of life of which we each are a part.

Quite a contrast from what passes as preparation today. Modern man races off to the driving range, where he unconsciously strikes out at a few balls, but in reality all he is doing is grooving old, dysfunctional patterns and reinforcing the neuroses that are not only inhibiting his experience of life but also shielding him from a direct experience of himself, while at the same time he tries to convince himself that he is actually practicing mastery.

The old man turned me back to face the valleys again, which I now saw as a series of vast labyrinths and spirals covered in green. "Each hole you play out here," he said, pointing one by one to each of the other eight hills, "will require a deeper level of surrender on your part, a letting go of something old to make space for something new. On each tee you will surrender a mask and a plate of armor so that by the end of the round all you'll have left to share with the world is your raw, beating heart. Everything you experience out here has been specifically designed to lead you back into the deeper dimensions of yourself."

Now he opened his hand, revealing the collection of rudraksha seeds he had brought with him. He looked at them for a moment, considering each in turn, then chose one and gave me the rest; I added them to the handful I had already secured away in my pocket.

He walked several steps away, crouched down, and laid the seed on the ground carefully, reverently. "We call this first tee the Altar of Life. By stepping out onto it, you anoint and initiate yourself for this journey of discovery." Then he waved his hand, beckoning me over to where he'd teed up the seed with a twig that was lying nearby.

I nodded but did not move. My bare feet felt planted right in the ground. I rubbed my sweaty palms on my pants and took a couple of deep breaths. The old man waved his hand again, and I took a step forward, then another and another until I stood only a few feet away from the seed. I looked at it and then at him.

"From this point of view," the old man said, standing up, "anything is possible. This is where it all starts." He nodded at the seed. "This ball represents the innocence, purity, and uniqueness of your own intentions. Your swing at this stage of the journey will reflect the many divided thoughts and internal conflicts that are not yet integrated realities for you; the force behind the swing is the aspiration to grow into this profound understanding. This is what we are all swinging for: a deeper connection to life and to ourselves."

As I stood there pondering all he had said, my old friend reached up into a nearby tree, removed a branch, and began to carve it meticulously. He was so absorbed in his task that I dared not interrupt him. When he was through, he handed me the instrument he had carved as if it were a sword. I studied it for quite some time, feeling the light and love that had gone into creating it. I began to feel as if everything that I had ever done for others, every act of random kindness within my life, was now contained within this ancient club. He stepped back and indicated it was time for me to step up to the tee. Another deep breath, and before I knew it, the seed sat at my feet. I looked around me, taking in the many sights, sounds, and smells: the majestic mountains, the rushing of the rivers, the hint of jasmine and incense that had followed me all the way here. I let the vibrations of these ancient hills and valleys enter my being, and it opened me up, preparing me for the trials to come.

Then I took my first swing, and it was filled with all my hopes and dreams, conscious and subconscious, casting into the wind every ounce of hope I had.

SEVEN

I stayed on the first hole for what seemed like an eternity. But it didn't worry me. This happened to most people, the old man had told me before he'd wandered off, back to his little hut, leaving me there alone with the game. We must be as clear and conscious as possible when we step into the next valley, and that's difficult to do, so we must take our time here, practicing our swing and getting it right.

The first swing on this Altar of Life and into the Valley of Hope represents a reckless abandonment of all the many beliefs, techniques, and superstitions we have accumulated and inherited throughout our lives. In releasing those, we allow our most radical aspirations to make their way up through our hearts, take shape, and find their true form within the flight of the ball. The first swing at life originates from an open, innocent place, one that is free from any guilt or remorse. This is where we find the courage within ourselves to ask for everything, to dare to dream.

Ironically, on this hole above all others, you are blessed if you have more strokes; you're not looking to birdie or bogey it, as either would be an attempt on your part to manipulate the game—unfortunately a very common theme in the lives of most initiates. Also, swinging and missing are, after all, very essential parts of the human experience. There's as much to be learned from what we perceive as failure as there is from success. Fortunately, when the ball gets blown off course, each moment in life offers us another swing, another chance to take a good look at our hopes and dreams and what we missed along the way.

So what did I see when I looked? First and foremost that out here, unlike in the "civilized" world, there was no scorecard. There was no keeping track of how much I had and if it was more or less than the next guy's. I could swing as much as I wanted or needed to, and I would not be penalized for taking too many or too little. We all have our own ways of keeping score in life and with each other, but in the end the only score that really matters is how much you have learned about yourself, how much you have grown into the life you've been given, and how much you now have to share with others. I could have spent hours, days, even weeks on this one hole if I wanted to—even a lifetime, though I hoped that would not be the case. Time was irrelevant in the valley of the gods. All that mattered was becoming my true self, which could be done only by letting go of the roles I played in life and the masks I wore. This, of course, brought my career as a caddy immediately to mind. Unfortunately, working in a service business, I often wore one different mask after another just to deal with the masks the players wore. There was a tendency on my part to go along in order to get along, and as a result I would spend four or five hours with people and never really get to know who they were, which in turn made it very difficult to muster any kind of genuine enthusiasm for their game or their lives, for that matter. In the golf world there is a tendency for assistants to overextend themselves, and I was as guilty of it as the next caddy. I began to see how I had betrayed my true self by trying to appease the illusions of others.

This was not the only way in which I was hiding myself,

though. Like many people, I tend to try to make myself sound like an authoritative figure—like someone who is in control and knows exactly what he's doing. I now realized that was another mask I wore as a defense mechanism, out of an unwillingness to show how vulnerable and insecure I really was, how unable I was to expose my heart to life.

Here there were no such veils. Though my innermost being protested at first—not wanting to be exposed, he held on to my masks and armor as tightly as he could—as I began to shed the costumes and layers of self I had been piling up one by one throughout my life, I discovered a truth: that the divine is within each one of us, and all we see, feel, and experience while traveling the paths of our lives reflects that divinity. From the lightest of the light to the darkest of the dark, God, the universe, the higher power—whatever one calls this guiding force—rests in every molecule, every cell, of everything that exists on Earth.

It was on this first fairway that I began the process of truly getting to know myself, and in doing so I began to access my own inner nature. I say "began" because this is a lifelong process that involves not only claiming the divine inside but also breaking down bit by bit the many illusions we all carry. My first step was to realize that I cannot give up on myself or on life no matter how hard it gets; I must not only face the uncomfortable and the unfamiliar and stay the course no matter what but also be willing to lean into it. This means not just dealing with but fully experiencing the frustration of swinging again and again and not getting it right, of not being able to control the ball or life for that matter. It is only in the depths of that helpless feeling that I can start to learn what trust truly is—trust of myself, the game of life, and the universe around me. Finally I could trust that the process will bring me where I need to be and that the hopes and dreams that I launched into the air here and the wishes each swing carried would incarnate later in the round and blossom within another valley, when I least expected it.

With this realization I was able to release myself from the first tee and enter the Valley of Hope, where the seeds of our dreams are planted, and our intentions become crystallized. My mind began to reflect the clarity of the clear mountain skies and would remain that way lest I wished to go back the way I came; if you enter this valley thinking about the fight you had with your partner or how many bills you have to pay, you're taking yourself out of the game of life, and that was the last thing I wanted to do. Instead I focused on the clean, crisp air that filled my lungs, the soft, rich earth beneath my feet, the cool breeze at my back that kept me moving forward.

My hike through the Valley of Hope gave me time to reflect on what I had learned on the first tee, to remember each swing, each wish, each attempt to expand my vision of life. The purity of these thoughts, the hope with which they filled my being, propelled me up the next hill so quickly that I barely saw the scenery as I passed it, and before I knew it I stood before the second stone temple, its prayer flags flying in the wind, the midmorning sun reflecting off the bells mounted at the top.

Atop this mighty hill was the second hole, known to our ancestors as the Mountain of Joy. This hole is all about bearing witness to the majesty of existence; it's about seeing the beauty of creation in all its many forms while also enjoying the adventure we weave through the tapestries of our lives. It's about oneness, about bringing together nature and humanity. At this hole we glorify what the gods have given us through creating harmonious lives for ourselves, existences that complement instead of work against the natural flow of things.

However, we also learn here to see the humor in ourselves and the world around us, to laugh at the absurdity of it all instead of letting it drag us down. Unfortunately too many of us take ourselves far too seriously. Our definition of self is limited to our masks and our fragmented personalities, which we have misinterpreted as who we truly are. By seeing ourselves as separate from life, by investing so much of our energy into who we think we are, we not only distort the inherent clarity within our souls, but we also miss out on the magic to be found along the way. There is a cosmic drama unfolding right before our eyes, and we can all play parts in it if only we accept the invitation.

Looking out over the valleys of the gods again, I took a new rudraksha seed from my pocket and held it in my hand. I felt its connection to my surroundings but also to all the things in this world that brought joy to my heart: the gentle breeze that was whispering through the leaves, the morning sunlight that now airbrushed the mountains with a golden light, and all of the many smiles that strangers had given to me along my way. This released a tremendous amount of anxiety that I hadn't even really been aware I held inside, and as I watched a pair of eagles soar by, their enormous wings spread wide, I felt as though I could launch myself into the wind with them if only I could shed the remaining weight of my past that held me to the ground.

Turning back toward the temple, I went over and teed up my seed. This new ball, as at the first hole, was a new intention and a new level of consciousness, a new dimension of human experience. I could feel that each swing would draw me closer to my next integration point. The joy this thought brought me was the joy of simply being alive, the thrill of laying this groundwork that would help me clarify my intentions and awaken my sense of purpose. Crouched down there, my hand still on the seed, I felt my life begin to unfold before me. I saw the trillions of possible experiences there were to choose from and understood how I would draw the ones that were meant for me to me as if I were a magnet. These experiences would ultimately shape the journey of my soul, for the "seek and ye shall find" principle is the foundation for the lives we all are attempting to live.

I stood up and took my first swing. It wasn't perfect, but nothing is in life. It's all about learning and growing, accepting and moving on. I took a few deep breaths and with them found a rhythm deep within myself, a steady heartbeat to guide me as I tried again. My next swing was smoother, less fragmented, and I felt the many energetic channels in my body opening up, creating a clear and unified pathway toward whatever would come next.

#

Before my guide had left me at the first hole, he had told me to approach each hole on the course with a refreshed and open state of mind. That was why there was at least a mile's walk from the green to the next tee—to give one time to reflect, to go over what was learned on the previous hole and prepare for the next. In our modern game of golf, there is a very short distance from green to tee, and unfortunately many of us race around the course, looking for excuses and avoiding opportunities to take responsibility for our lives. Out here one is looking not only for the next tee but also the next dimension of human experience, for each hole represents a quantum leap in one's own development.

Before the third hole I came upon an enormous gate—an energetic portal, actually, through which I had to pass to continue my game. The beggar in Ranikhet had told me that in order to proceed from valley to valley I had to reach a certain level of integrity, for out here one is constantly raising the bar in terms of one's own authenticity. I had to have a firm and grounded expression of who I was. I stood before the third tee nervous and in awe, unsure of what to do. What if I wasn't ready? What would happen? Would the gate zap me somewhere else—maybe back to New York, like this had all been a dream?

But this was all nonsense, this worrying, because I would never find out what would happen unless I gave it a try. If I was ready, I would pass through and go on to the third tee. If I wasn't then I'd take whatever the universe saw fit to give me. If it meant ending up back where I had started, so be it. I could always try again. If it meant being stuck in the same place for a while, I could handle that too.

See? There's always a solution, I told myself and then closed my eyes. I took a deep breath, lifted my foot, and stepped forward… and when I opened my eyes, I found myself on the other side of the gate. There'd been no zapping, no setback, no transporting me to another time and place, which meant one thing: I was ready. I tried not to pat myself on the back, but the thought did give me a little rush.

Beyond the gate lay a fertile valley, one of the many I had seen from the top of the last mountain. Everything was an emerald green—the leaves on the trees, the grass beneath my bare feet—and the air was so absolutely silent I could almost hear the drops of dew dripping off the foliage that surrounded me. As I passed through the valley, I could see the rishis' original blueprint of this enormous course: the mountains as the teeing grounds, the valleys the fairways, the terraces cut into the sides of the mountains the putting greens. They set the whole thing up in a very meticulous way, incorporating all elements of the landscape to create vortexes of energy that could work on a man's psyche in the most subtle ways, leading him forward while helping him to look within himself and examine what needed to be worked on there.

These ancient seers, the original architects, possessed profound knowledge of the universe and a deep understanding of sacred geometry, which they incorporated into every aspect of their designs. They chose this location and the layout of the course so carefully, with an awareness of how the surrounding land and the vistas seen from each tee would intersect with the structures of the human eye, setting off energetic signals and activating geometric patterns within the human form that could alter one's magnetic field and vibratory rate, influencing the degree to which one was open. Such shifts in consciousness have propelled men to seek higher frequencies and establish deeper senses of balance within themselves, which is in many ways what this game is really all about: each hole has a way of addressing imbalance by realigning and reunifying the heart and the head, the masculine and the feminine, the left and right sides of the brain, and ultimately the kingdoms of Heaven and Earth that coexist within the human form.

Following this course, I now realized, was like following a road map back to my own true self, as in each valley and on every hill I was forced to examine myself more closely than I ever had. Understanding the map meant knowing what each hole and valley represented and that the vibration of each fairway had a distinct and specific purpose. It meant understanding that everything has a relationship to everything else and that with every level of expansion comes another level of examination. The very path that sets you free in life is the one that ultimately requires the most attention, for the ego does not simply roll over and surrender. It fights right up to the end to try to save its old forms of reality.

At the end of the fertile valley, I approached the base of yet another hill. This one was higher and steeper than the last, as the last had appeared higher and steeper than the first. With the shift in altitude, I gasped and wheezed my way up to the top, but no matter how difficult it became, I kept going. I remembered the words of the old man in the hut, who had told me that in order to proceed through this game, there had to be a full commitment to oneself. I knew it would take time, but I was determined to take and overcome whatever this path threw at me. I had to; it was the only way to set myself free.

EIGHT

The third hole in the rishis' game of golf is called Clarity, though this is an interesting paradox as it is located on the dark side of the mountain, an area where the sun rarely shines. Within this darkness, though, comes the opportunity to expose our shadows and doubts, the secrets that we hold within, the many ways in which we say no to life and sabotage our true selves. There is nowhere to hide here, and we can look only within ourselves for direction and guidance, as anything outside of us will lead to only more doubt and confusion.

The tee is perched on the edge of a cliff on the third hill, overlooking the valleys and the rivers that run through them. Standing there with another new rudraksha seed in my grip, I could see everything I had already been through and much of what was to come. The air was sweet and fresh, free of the pesticides and pollutants of the cities below, and I breathed it deeply into my lower belly and then exhaled deeply, letting go of all the stale energy and random thoughts I'd accumulated. This is called belly breathing, something I had learned in the temple on Koh Phangan, which over time changes not only the configuration of the brain but the human form as well. It creates a deep integration that helps generate new neurological pathways and enabled the oxygen in the pure, high-altitude atmosphere to flow deeper into my cells, bringing a renewed sense of clarity and allowing me to reconnect once again with my purpose in life.

The third hole is very powerful and must be approached with a tremendous amount of respect as well as self-respect, and I kept that in mind as I teed up my seed. This was where I would build my self-confidence and develop the courage I would need to overcome whatever might lie ahead by fully accepting all aspects of myself and in doing so loosen my grip on the illusion that I was separate from life. When we think of ourselves this way—as living in the world but not as part of it—we foster in ourselves a sense of unworthiness that in turn creates all the shadows and doubts that plague us, that keep us from reaching the Promised Land. This is the lie of separation: that we can somehow stand outside of life, control our own experiences, and engineer our own awakenings.

Understandably, many who play this game become lost at this point. Unable or unwilling to acknowledge and experience those dark places within themselves, they turn back to the illusions and dysfunctions they've held for so long simply because they feel safer and more certain there than with whatever unknowns might lie ahead. The realizations we find here can be overwhelming as they begin to strike at the heart of each illusion upon which we have, up to this point, based our realities. But within that darkness and those shadows we can also find many hidden resources—power that we never knew we had or that we've previously overlooked or even dismissed. In tantra it's said that what we pursue is really a dark knowledge and a place where the bottom falls out and you realize that you actually don't know anything. If you face it head on, you'll soon see that darkness is actually a fuller expression of life than the light is.

Upon this green we initiate and empower ourselves through

surrendering our own versions of reality; we come to realize that up until this point, all we have really been doing was managing our masks. We realize we are divine, and there is divinity within us. It then becomes easy to see those who have no self-respect as they have masked their divinity with false courage, hiding behind arrogance and aggression.

I had fallen victim to this. In the darkness I re-experienced all the anger and rage I had felt in the past toward those who had disappointed me and toward myself for not living a full life, for allowing myself to get caught up in other people's drama because I was too lazy to engage my own life fully and unwilling to trust myself. I felt a new anger as well, from realizing I had overextended myself into the realities of others because I wanted to be liked and accepted, but this was another lie. If I couldn't accept myself, the world was not going to swoop in and do it for me.

Within the darkness I was able to see that much of what I had put out into the world and given to others had come from my mind, not my heart, and in truth it was manipulative. I was giving to get instead of giving just for the joy of being able to do so. This is the way of much of the world, unfortunately, and that misguided, greedy mindset has brought us to the state we are in today: Our oceans are polluted, and our rainforests are almost gone because we've cut them down. We hunt and kill animals for pleasure, and even human life seems to hold no value. We go to war and slaughter each other over and over and over again.

Moving through all this anger led me to a place of grief and sadness more profound than I had ever felt. I saw the human race for the tragedy it is, as a gluttonous automaton that crushes every small thing that gets in its way. And though I liked to consider myself one of its victims—an outsider, not a part of the whole—that was another lie. In truth I was part of the machine. In this darkness I could fully acknowledge that I was not only the victim; I was also the crime.

If we can stay connected and focused here, and swing with clarity, we will not only connect with our own truths but find that the place we swing from and the target we aim for are actually one and the same. As I played the game, I felt my heart center—the fourth of the seven chakras, or the centers in our bodies through which energy flows—opening; each successive swing opened it a little further until I almost felt like I would burst. In that empty space was nothing but untapped energy, and I felt it coursing through my body. I was now ready to open to new realities and move toward new opportunities while always remaining humble and fully accepting myself for the person I already was.

With this realization I was able to birdie the hole, which meant I was ready to proceed onward.

#

The fourth hill was once again steeper than the last, and again I had to acclimate myself to the elevation. By the time I reached the top and leaned against the wall of the ancient temple there, I was out of breath and lightheaded.

"Sit and rest," I heard someone say. "This game may not be forced. Each tee is an opportunity to expand your horizons and your definitions of reality in your own time and in your own way."

I jumped at the sound of the voice. Turning around in a circle, I finally found its source: it was the old man from the hut, my guide who had brought me to the first hole.

"What are you doing here?" I asked, unsure if he was real or just a figment of my oxygen-starved imagination.

He bowed his head to me in greeting and then looked back up again. "I am here to show you where the next hole is."

I smiled. Another lesson from this sage was just what I needed at the moment—something to pull me out of the dark place that had trailed me from the previous hole.

"Please," I said, taking a seat on the hard-packed dirt. "Go on."

The old man paced for a moment, a hand on his chin as he gathered his thoughts. Then he stopped and dropped down to sit cross-legged in front of me.

"This hole is called the Promised Land," he began, a tone of exhilaration in his voice. "You see the landing area is flat, and the playing field is even. This is because a Promised Land shows no favoritism. No matter if you're rich or poor, old or young, sick or healthy, all are welcome here. But make no mistake: there are still hazards to face, for the truth and integrity that you have found within yourself will soon be tested by the light you are now approaching. In this game, as in life, there will always be some sort of obstacle to overcome, for nothing good comes to us without work. Look out over the valley."

He swept his arm out, gesturing to the land below and beyond this hill. I leaned over the edge and took a look.

"You'll see there is water to the left and sand on the right," he continued. "And the fairway is narrower than the others have been. This is the gauntlet we all must pass through in order to rid ourselves of the illusions we've clung to about ourselves—and shed them. The traps are the illusions that have up to this point defined our existence and dictated our reality. They represent the many places in life where we get stuck. I have spent lifetimes in those traps and know each one of them intimately. You will fully encounter the gravitational pull of your past here and will have to face the road ahead with tremendous courage, for on it you will face your own self-deceptions, and all of the many things that you have hidden from yourself will begin to surface."

He paused and smiled kindly. He held his hands out, palms up, indicating the space around us. "This is where you wave good-bye to all of your favorite fairy tales."

I tried to smile, too, but the idea was daunting to me. I had given up so much of myself so far I wasn't sure what was left. Would I completely lose myself here? Would I become someone else?

The old man shook his head as if he could read my thoughts. "To reach this land you have already made a promise to stay true to yourself. Now you must stay focused, or you will quickly lose yourself within the clouds of your own illusions. This is one of the major problems with the human race today: we have accumulated far too much useless information, and it swims around in our heads, creating unnecessary noise and static that obscure the signals and messages that come from the depths of our being. We cannot focus on one thing at a time, and this is one of the biggest stumbling blocks in our current phase of evolution."

I laughed. If a man who lived in a hut out in the wilderness could see this about us, how come we have so much trouble seeing it in ourselves? We are constantly multitasking, "concentrating" on two, three, four things at a time. We're on the phone and the Internet; the TV blares in the background. We're working, but we're also making reservations for some chic new destination that everyone is talking about and then tweeting and posting it to make our friends jealous. We think this is "staying in touch," but these social mediums we've created are nothing but manifestations of how unwilling and unable we are to communicate directly with one another. We hedge ourselves with unending streams of useless information and incessant activity, and as a result we marginalize the power and magnitude of the present moment. We assume imagined identities in attempts to cover up the vast emptiness that underlies our existence.

"Before we can land on this fairway," my guide went on, "we must look at all the many ways in which we hide, deflect, and pull back from life and how unwilling we are to give the present moment the attention it deserves. We must also identify and fully face all the lies we have accumulated in order to prop up our realities. It is impossible even to attempt to play out this hole without an acute sense of awareness. The narrow fairway demands focus and will command all of your attention. Here you will get a chance to really see how much you trust not only your swing but your own life as well, for the swing is simply a reflection of the life and the path you have chosen."

He stood slowly and pulled a rudraksha seed from his pocket. He held it in his fist as he walked from one end of the ledge to the other. "This hole, unlike all the others, has two tees. The forward tee…" He stopped and bent down, setting up another twig tee, as he had at the first hole. "Is for those who did not birdie on the previous hole." He smiled at me. "So that one will not apply to you. Those who did not birdie the third hole are still locked in unteachable patterns. They are far too invested in their illusions of individuality and bound by the perceived separations that prevent them from advancing. Their hearts are not yet open, and they are trapped by the mechanics of their own techniques. So this will be merely a practice hole for them."

He placed his seed on the tee and looked at it, crouched down close, his thin body folded in against itself. "Those who did not birdie the previous hole do not know they carry the divine inside themselves. Unfortunately this is how many people on this planet live. They may believe in the divine, but faith and belief are not the same thing. Faith is knowing from within, whereas belief is guessing and trying to know. Belief creates the separation and sets up the duality from which you believe you are never good enough to enter the Promised Land; faith unifies our divided selves. Belief is doubt, and it's through that lens that you filter your focus. A swing grounded in belief will reflect the conflicts and neuroses of your divided self, and your indecisive mind and scattered thoughts will create strong crosswinds to throw your ball off course.

"As you gaze out onto that narrow fairway in the distance, your focus will not be on the flagstick; rather it will be drawn to the water or the sand. Basically your doubts will be trying to decide which hazard they would rather land in and which illusion your beliefs would be more comfortable with. Doubt creates nothing but distraction and will sabotage your best intentions if you are not fully grounded in faith. These doubts create a tremendous imbalance within the body, which is why you see so many people fidgeting not only over the ball but through their lives as well."

He stood up again and turned away from the tee, stretching his back as he looked out over the remaining valleys. "Those who start from the forward tee," he continued, coming back over toward me, "must attempt to play out the hole nonetheless. They must meditate on the ball, and over time they will come to see that up until now they have been following other people's balls, believing other people's beliefs and realities. We have inherited all our beliefs from others, and none of them has related to our own spiritual adventures. You will never make it through the clouds by following the truth, the ball, or the beliefs of another. It is only with an open heart and your own ball of truth that you can ever enter the Promised Land."

He came back in front of me and produced another rudraksha seed from his pocket. He leaned over and handed it to me. I stood up, too, and made my way to the fourth tee. As I took my first swing, he continued to speak.

"If you are not yet a master of your life, you are simply walking through existence, believing in illusions of who you think you are. And this will be as far as you can go for now. Life is mastery, and the joy of life is found in becoming your own master. For the ones who are mastering themselves, the Promised Land opens up; it welcomes you home. Do you feel the wind at your back?"

I swung again and watched the ball sail off high and straight, with no crosscurrents to drift it either way. I turned to the old man and nodded my head.

"Now you are no longer forcing your way through life against the winds of your own ignorance," he said. "Only those who are truly at peace and on target with themselves can continue to ascend the spiral and make their way down the Golden Road."

He remained in silence for a while, watching me play. I took one slow swing after another, the ball's path always holding straight and true. With each soaring leap it took, I felt myself opening up wider again, accepting not just who I was at that moment but that I could choose who to be: the lost wanderer or an active participant in my own game of life. I focused on that idea; I honed it in my mind until it became a part of me, until I believed—no, I had faith— that no matter what hazards I faced, I could surpass them and keep moving on.

At the end of the fairway, my guide finally spoke again.

"From here on your point of view will change again as dramatically as the landscape that awaits your discovery. There will be no more sand, no more water, only rolling hills with intricate, subtle contours, covered with wild grasses of unimaginable colors. You will see no villages along the way, for the vibrations of these valleys are too strong and refined for most mortals."

He reached out and touched my arm, with that warm, soothing smile on his face once again. "The remaining holes will present you with many new opportunities, for everything now is in play, and there is nowhere to lose yourself within this game of life.

There is no longer anything in your life that is out of bounds. In fact there are no boundaries to cross. Any that you had were merely impositions of your own ego and the limitations your conditional mind had placed on your awareness. You will bear no such burdens now. You are no longer blocked by the judgments, beliefs, and incomplete perceptions that bind most souls to mortality and their very limited realities. All of life patiently waits for you to arrive. Each moment is a gateway, a portal into a deeper dimension of yourself, and there is no need to place your belief and hope in a better world. There is no better world, only the one you live in here and now."

How wonderful would that be, I thought, to focus only on the present? To put all my faith and energy into making this experience the fullest it can be? I longed to surrender to it, to that idea that there was a living totality that is constantly blooming and blossoming and unfolding within myself, that the freedoms of discovery, creativity, and expression were mine for the taking. I had enjoyed my experiences thus far; I had done many interesting and fulfilling things. But I had never experienced the true joy of living a full and complete life, of existing within that totality and within the world simultaneously. That this was now attainable felt like a gift—one that I could give myself.

"The remaining holes will be challenging," the old man said, bringing my thoughts back down to earth. "But you are a master, so even if you play them poorly, you will never be defeated. Each perceived failure will only help you improve how you play your own game of life. You will take full responsibility for your own existence, and in doing so you will grow into the realization that everything in the universe lies within the same sacred circle of life you also inhabit. There will be no guru, no teacher, no guide, no other master. You will now walk alone, and that aloneness will awaken the totality of life."

The old man stepped back, leaving me to stand alone at the foot of the next mountain.

"The first four holes were for the student, the devotee, the disciple," he said, his voice receding behind me. "Once you step on the fifth tee, you are playing with the gods."

NINE

My guide called me a master; I wasn't sure I was ready to accept that title yet. I had come so far since I'd begun this journey, and I certainly wasn't the same person I had been when I had started to play the game. I'd shed a few masks and much of the armor that had protected me and kept me from fully engaging with the world and with myself. Still, I felt, I had so much to learn.

I turned back toward my guide, sensing he was about to leave me. "I'm not ready."

He approached and laid his ancient hand on my shoulder, a reassuring gesture. His skin was like a dried husk, his hand a weightless whisper brushing against the cloth of my shirt.

"Remember, you play this game at your own pace," he told me, guiding me away from the foot of the mountain off to a group of boulders to the side. He sat down on one; I sat down next to him. "If you feel you are not ready to move on, you can practice your swing here on the fourth hole for as long as you'd like. This is as far as I can take you, for we are reaching a place where words no longer apply."

I looked out over the fairway through which I'd just passed, at the traps and hazards that surrounded it. This hadn't been an easy hole. Did I really want to do a repeat performance?

Better the devil you know, I thought, the old adage popping into my head. I looked over at the old man. "Are they all like this? I mean the holes—do they just keep getting harder and harder as the game goes on?"

He stuck out his bottom lip and frowned, a sort of "maybe yes, maybe no" gesture. "I cannot say one hole is hard and one is easy," he said. "They are all different from one another, and they mean different things to different people. What you consider difficult might be the easiest thing in the world for someone else."

He looked at me for a moment, narrowing his eyes, considering me. "But I understand your trepidation. So I will give you a brief outline of the next five holes," he said, "and you can decide how hard they are."

I nodded and settled myself in for another lesson.

"The remaining holes," he began, "are all named after colors, as each of the fairways reflects a different ray of light. This perfect rainbow represents the five rays of divinity that live and breathe within you, and you will play each hole as a separate aspect of that divinity. In knowing these aspects of yourself, you will realize there is only one omnipotent god, and it is you. You are the pot of gold at the end of the rainbow—you in all your glory and mastery and clarity, with all your love for the divine within."

He looked up at the mountain next to us, its top hidden in the clouds. "The fifth hole," he said, "is called Magenta. The rishis called this section of the course the Gates of the Sun because when you enter the realm of the gods, anything within you that still clings to its own version of reality will burn away as if scorched by the sun. If you are out here only for yourself, not for all of humanity, then you will never make it through these golden gates, nor will those who are overly preoccupied with their own sense of safety and security. Such people will never even find their way to this part of the course."

He lowered his gaze, holding his hands out in front of him as if imagining the scene he was about to describe. "As you step onto the fifth tee, you will find yourself in a different world, one that radiates a quality of light unlike anything you've ever seen. The many interpretations of life that we all cling to from time to time are now just beliefs and illusions that belong to the past and no longer apply to the reality you are now a part of. You can now fully embrace the universe and approach life with all the joy and passion that has long been buried deep down inside your soul. Accompanying this freedom is a profound silence that radiates from the depth of your being. This is the true feeling of coming home, of being able to say for the first time that you are part of the universe. A great feeling of acceptance unfolds, and you are now able just to go with the flow. All struggles and separations of the ego are well behind you, and the oneness you have grown into continues to expand exponentially."

The old man looked at me. "The rest I cannot tell you."

I laughed, thinking he was joking. But his face remained somber. "What?" I asked. "Why?"

"Because, as I said before, your experience out here is yours alone. No other person who plays the game of life will walk the same fairways that you do. The remaining holes reflect this."

I rubbed my chin, looking back out at the narrow fairway of hole four. Maybe I had been right—maybe they would all be like that one. Now I felt more apprehension than ever.

"I can, however, tell you the colors of the remaining holes, their reflecting rays of focus, and the intentions which they represent."

I let out a relieved sigh and then thanked him, and he continued on.

"The translucent colors that emanate from the remaining fairways will directly impact your being in very profound ways like rays of sunlight through a clear prism. As the light penetrates to the depths of your being, it will crystallize and magnify the many holograms within the human form, simultaneously awakening the many dimensions of existence you have previously blocked, shut down, or ignored. Up until now you have spent a tremendous amount of energy on evading, denying, and deflecting the richness, complexity, and multiplicity of the human experience, which is your true inheritance."

He pointed up toward the next hole again. "Once you reach the fifth fairway, you are free to receive and experience the person you really are as these reflections of the light accelerate a process that began long ago. You will no longer be trapped within the realms of name and form, nor will you be preoccupied with karmic patterns that need to be unwound. Instead you will notice flowers you have never seen before, scents you have never smelled, and sounds that are completely unfamiliar to the human ear. This assault on the senses, which is a direct result of the quality of light that shines not only through the fairway but through you as well, will help you fully open up to the vastness of the ever-expanding universe."

"Sounds like what happened to me in your hut," I said, remembering that dizzy, spinning feeling I'd experienced as my mind and body fought along the fine line between my imagined self and the universe.

The old man nodded. "Something like that but on a much greater scale." He paused, gazing out at nothing in particular. When he continued, his voice was distant. "There is a profound intensity to be found in these remaining valleys, and unless your soul is able to let go of its own version of reality, you will not be able to handle it." Looking over at me, he came back to the present. "That night in my hut, you had some glimpses of this vast reality, but you pulled back and shut down from it because your ego was not yet ready to let go. This fifth fairway triggers a great awakening process as the rays of light open up new dimensions, each of which is another avenue of experience and expression within you. Your cells will vibrate at a frequency that supersedes anything within the third dimension. And it is through this alchemy of light that you will begin to truly discover the universe."

"What about the ball?" I asked, feeling in my pocket for my last few rudraksha seeds. Finding one, I took it out and showed it to him.

"There is only one ball left to be played here," he said, his smile now a magical blend of mischief and wisdom, "and that is you. Out here it doesn't matter if you are a drunk, a junkie, a gambler, a sinner, or a saint—whatever your illusions or vices, here you will see with clarity that these habits and hobbies are just toys on the playground in your game of life. The key is to learn to establish yourself in the light of your own unique truth. When you can do that, all gates open up. Those who cannot are forced to return to the first tee and start over with whatever tools and insights they might have found along the way. The light pushes back against any foolish souls who try to force their way out here; it dismantles them to the point that they collapse back into their own illusions of ignorance, arrogance, and greed, and as a result they are unable to proceed."

"Sinners in the hands of an angry god?" I asked, remembering the title of the old Christian sermon, full of vivid images of hell and damnation.

My guide looked amused. "Perhaps. The universe, and each course one attempts to navigate in life, has its wrathful aspects, but all in all you will find out here that life originates from a very benevolent place. Ultimately you arrived here as the result of your own intentions, worked out through the course of your life in the many decisions you made and the actions you took. If those decisions and actions were based in greed and arrogance…" He shrugged. "Everything comes with its consequences."

With that we were silent for a while. My old friend closed his eyes and meditated, and I followed suit. Closing my eyes, I put my hands on my knees and breathed deeply in…and out…and in again. On my exhales I focused on one word in my mind: clarity, or acceptance, or simply open.

"Are you ready to continue?" the old man asked gently after some time, and I opened my eyes. Everything seemed brighter than before, somehow more alive. I nodded and smiled, and he returned the gestures.

"The sixth hole is called Sky Blue," he said, "and you can play it in any way you wish. This might sound easy enough, but it's a difficult thing for many people even to imagine, so few make it that far. Most souls can't quite grasp the freedom that comes from surrendering the illusions of the ego, and as a result they find themselves living in a very conditional reality. Most misunderstand this freedom I speak of. It is not a freedom from the life you are currently living; rather it is a freedom that includes everything, and only within such a freedom will you ever find the capacity to be who you truly are. Those who can accept this freedom find on the sixth fairway their ability to directly experience the world from a place that is open, clear, and free from separation—as part of the world itself. In this state you can see not only the world and its infinite possibilities but also all of the many horrific conditions that exist; you will hear the cries of suffering, the moans of the sick, the pleas of the weak. Do not turn away. These are the same sounds Jesus heard on the side of the mountain and Buddha from under the bodhi tree. Weep like they did. Let loose your tears of compassion, for it is through them that you can begin to open the door to the awakened state and the lotus of wisdom each soul carries within."

He got up from his seat on the rock and stretched out his back, raising his arms high into the sky as on that morning when I had seen him welcoming the day outside his hut. Then he began to walk, a quick look back over his shoulder the only clue that I was to follow him. I jumped up.

"Hole number seven is called Violet," he began, meandering along the green, his hands clasped behind his back. "This is where the creator in you begins to emerge. As you make your way into the violet valley, you open up to the deeper levels of your soul, and all of your long-forgotten talents and gifts and the latent capacities of your being begin to awaken. Only through a true awareness of the self can we even begin to unlock the wisdom of the creative genius within, and this is where the process starts."

I thought of what talents I had that might emerge. I'd never been too good at painting or playing music; my writing, I suppose, is not that bad. Perhaps I was meant to be a caddy. In all honesty I had no idea what might emerge, and that was because I had lived so out of touch with my soul for so very long.

"There has always been a universal law of energy," my old friend continued. "It states on Earth there is a state of consciousness that we can call heaven, and everything we store in there—our talents, our skills—can never be lost. When you have served the planet well and used your gifts in the service of others, those gifts stay with you forever; they are energies that become recycled and reincarnated back into your next birth. These are the karmic patterns that go into forming the shape and trajectory of your next life, your next game. They will influence your swing and dictate the flight of the ball along with all the future realities you'll encounter on the course. The child prodigy who walks upon the Earth is simply picking up where he or she left off last time around."

"And those who choose not to serve man?" I asked. "What happens to them in their next lives?"

"Those who serve only their own egos are left with no heavenly stores to carry with them on into their future lives. And their egos—the only thing they can be said to truly possess—die with them, so what is left? Nothing but unrefined insights that will keep them swinging again and again at that first hole but never advancing until they realize they are not separate from others. The judgments and beliefs we have about ourselves and others bind us to this wheel of karma and the experience of mortality."

We had reached a copse of trees in the meadow that surrounded the fairway—a stand of enormous evergreens with blue berries, rudraksha seeds littering all the ground below. After clearing off a space with his foot, the old man sat down in the shade of one of the trees, and I did the same.

"There is a hidden valley within the violet fairway," he said, "that leads out onto a meadow not unlike this one. But the violet meadow is special because it connects these mountains to many other ranges. This is where the old souls and practical mystics of the mountains meet for creative collaboration, where those who have chosen to serve the world come to reconnect. Only those who are fully committed to the service of others will ever find their way to this hidden part of the course, but those who do will find themselves among kindred souls. Their meadows will be filled with people they have known for lifetimes and who, like them, have come back to serve."

I gazed up into the trees as he spoke, listening to the gentle patter of rudraksha seeds falling from the branches and hitting the ground. I could just see traces of blue sky through the evergreens' green needles, and the smell of the earth surrounded me.

"Some souls will stay on the violet fairways for quite some time," my guide continued, bringing my attention back to him, "spending their time looking back on the Earth from the expanses of an awakened nature, through the prism and lenses of compassion. And these people often use this multidimensional perspective to create new forms, new models, and dynamic solutions for the Earth. Have you heard of a woman named Emma Kunz?" I thought for a moment. "Swiss artist?" I asked. "Made outsider art, big on geometric abstraction?"

The old man nodded. "She was also a healer, and she passed through these metaphoric fairways in the 1950s. She created her mandalas while roaming these violet valleys, but man had not yet developed far enough to truly understand her work. Only those who are able to pass through the meadow of mystics and the violet valley can even attempt to interpret her work and her vision for the future of humanity accurately."

I thought about some pictures of her drawings I had seen. Incredibly intricate designs and patterns—nice to look at, but I'd never known there was any more to it than that. I made a note to look them up again when I left this place, to see what new levels I could interpret.

"Let's move on to the next hole," the old man said as he pushed himself up from the ground, and once again he walked while he spoke. "The eighth hole is called Emerald, and this is the hole of respect and gratitude. This is where you will learn to fully respect life in all its many forms because these emerald fields will awaken the love for all that is within your heart. You will no longer see people as separate from you, but you will see them as they see themselves. You will feel them as if they were cells within your own body. This is how true compassion emerges. All of these openings I speak of are very relative in a sense, for some may think their hearts are open because they don't want to kill anyone, but the heart center I speak of is more related to the heart of the Bodhisattva. This is the heart that says, 'I cannot imagine leaving here until everyone is awake.' For when the heart is truly open, we know we are everyone, and your compassion is then moved to anyone who is rambling around in the cities or villages below, lost in a blur of confusion."

Compassion. The word rolled around in my mind. I'd always thought I was a compassionate person, but was I really? I felt sorrow and empathy for those in need, those in pain whether psychic or physical. But what about those whose struggles were not so easy to see? I thought back on all the people I'd caddied for and how judgmental I was of them, quick to point out their egos and their annoying habits, their greed and self-centeredness. But I didn't really know them. Nor did I give them the time and space to reveal their true selves to me. Perhaps I was the one who was too wrapped up in my own ego, in the image I had of myself, which I'd thought was so different from these people's souls.

Now I knew that this separation was an illusion. Those golfers I'd detested, they were me, and I was them. All paths lead to God, it is said in the Bhagavad Gita—and God is everything and everyone. So that means we are all connected to one another. I don't know how I'd never seen this before.

"On the emerald fairway," my guide said, once again as if he could read my thoughts, "this unity becomes a living and breathing truth. It is no longer a wish or a dream. It's not a belief. It is reality."

By that time he had brought me back around to the base of the mountain. Looking up, I saw the clouds had cleared away, and bright sunshine illuminated the last temple above.

"We are at the last hole, my friend," he said. "The ninth hole is called Gold. This is the hole of mastery. Metaphorically speaking, the player who finds his way here has won the Masters." He gave me a sidelong glance and that radiant smile, obviously quite pleased with his joke. "There are, however, no green jackets, trophies, or acknowledgments to be found here, for one no longer feels the need to be validated by others. His deepest hopes, longings, and aspirations for himself and his life are fulfilled. He is now a god…the lord of his own life. For the first time he can honestly say there is nothing that exists outside of him, and this statement awakens a profound sense of humility.

"On the altar of the ninth tee, you get only one swing, for that is all that's necessary. With it you make your offering to the universe: your humility, a promise to serve others, profound gratitude to both those who have played this course before you and left their wisdom for you to discover and to those who have shown you the way."

I nodded, thinking back on all the help I've had along this journey: the beggar who brought me to the mountains, this old man who has been my guide and given me so much knowledge. The countless strangers along the way who shared their hearts and lives with me. But it goes back much further than that. What about Lance, who had told me to go to Koh Phangan? What about the childhood friend and his grandfather who brought me to their golf club way back when? What about all of the many people I had caddied for over the years? All these people and many others had set me on different paths in my life, some of which worked out and some that I was still working out.

"The course—and the journey, for that matter—does not end here," the old man went on. "Within your offering there is another opening, and from within that opening comes a directive from deep down inside. This is where your true destiny reveals itself. Some will be directed to hole out on nine and make their way back down the mountain, through the valleys, and into the cities and villages below. There they will serve the rest of humanity in the form of guides, or caddies, and in doing so they will have the privilege and the opportunity to share their love and wisdom as a pure expression of joy. Others will be directed to continue down the golden road and play on."

"Play on?" I asked, shaking my head. "I thought the ninth was the last hole."

The old man shook his head as well. "Really there are an infinite number of holes to be played, an infinite number of universes to experience, and an infinite number of ways to continually expand one's vision of life. There are so many roads and so many levels in which one can engage and experience life. And there is no end to the journey, for there is no limit to how much one can open up his or her heart to life. But there is one essential, underlying reality that holds the entire universe together, and it is consistent and ever present no matter which path you choose."

He stopped. I waited for him to continue, but he didn't—as if waiting for me to ask what it was.

"So?" I asked. "What is it?"

He smiled. "The reality is that each moment is another chance to get to know yourself a little bit better. Even though we're all on different holes, we do ultimately share the same course and play through the same game, which we have all come to call life. We are all on the road to being more conscious, and every moment along the way is a beginning—not a new beginning, because new implies the next moment is somehow more valuable than the last. The reality of life is that each step on the path is a realization in itself."

"So I can mess up today, but there's always tomorrow, and I can try again."

"In essence, yes. But you could also mess up, as you say, right now, and then right now you get another chance to get it right. Those who are far wiser than I am often remind me that in the end, we all go through ten thousand experiences—it's just a question of how quickly we want to play. Do you wish to experience yourself in one life or in ten thousand? That choice is always yours. That is the ultimate grace in this universe: that we get to choose, and our choices are simply the reflections of what we all hold deep down inside."

I looked up the face of the mountain again. The temple still stood out brightly on top, its prayer flags flapping in a gentle breeze as if beckoning me to come hither. I closed my eyes. Was I ready now?

Over the course of this game I had moved from density to clarity, from belief into faith, from doubt into knowing. Now it was time, I knew, to move from mortality into eternity.

"I'm ready," I said, and I turned to look for my friend. But I was too late. He had already disappeared into the mist of the evening sky.

Made in the USA
Middletown, DE
24 June 2018